May God
richly bless yo

Alfred Young

MW01531928

DIVINE STRATEGIES
FOR LIFE
IN TODAY'S WORLD

ALLYSON L. YOUNG, M.ED.

xulon PRESS

Divine Strategies for Life In Todays World
by Allyson L. Young, M.Ed.

Printed in the United States of America.

ISBN 9781498449205

www.xulonpress.com

CONTENTS

PREFACE

The inspiration for *Divine Strategies for Life in Today's World* came much by surprise. About a year ago, I started writing devotional messages, which I call "The Chaplain's Corner," for a weekly newsletter. As the devotional writings began to accumulate, I realized I could combine them into a book. In each writing, I use a consistent format to describe a real, relevant and sometimes challenging life scenario followed by a Scriptural text for life application, a prayer and Scripture focus. All are presented as a combined divine strategy that a believer can use to take a spiritual approach to confronting the issues described in the scenario.

Many readers of my weekly devotional told me how much they look forward to the devotional messages and how each provides solid answers for solving or coping with the challenging life issues they face during the week. God also began to illumine for me the principles that **prayer** and **Scripture application** are two specific spiritual warfare strategies that believers **MUST** use at the same time to combat the enemy effectively.

I am so thankful God has graced me to share these strategies with people everywhere to use as daily devotionals or as a reference to address specific circumstances. Pastors and church leaders may also use portions of the book as thought starters to further develop their divinely inspired sermons or sermonettes. Ministry teachers may use the book as a Sunday school or Bible study text for regular discussions.

Most of all, I hope readers will be comforted in knowing this promise from James 1:5, NRSV. "If any one of you is lacking in wisdom, ask God, who gives to all generously and ungrudgingly, and it will be given you."

Many thanks to my devoted husband, Derek, and our children. Apart from God, you all are my greatest inspiration!

--Allyson L. Young, M.Ed.

FOREWORD

As I look back over my life and consider all the people who have positively influenced me, they all have one thing in common. They demonstrate their care and concern on a consistent basis. Among all the people I know, no one lives a life of demonstrating care and concern for others like Allyson Young, my friend of 20 years, wife of 18 years, co-parent of 17 years (four children) and business partner of 10 years.

With a mission to "go about doing good" (Acts 10:38), she has been a constant example of what it means to live the Christian life. Through the good times, the not-so-good times and the "unable to understand what's going on" times, her faithfulness to the Word of God, the call of God and the people of God has been unwavering.

As a national motivational speaker, I have the great privilege of meeting thousands of men, women and youth from various backgrounds and locations across America. In considering many of their stories, problems, challenges and fears, Allyson's book, *Divine Strategies for Life in Today's World,* is just what many people seek. People need a clear, relevant resource that cuts to the chase of their issues with godly solutions.

In this book, Allyson shares her thoughts, feelings, perspectives and experiences and ultimately, the divine strategies that, she has applied in her life. These strategies will help others achieve victory in the face of life's many challenges. Each section, chapter and entry in this book provides a clear pathway to God's wisdom for living the Christian life and overcoming obstacles by using spiritual tools. I especially like that the book presents a nicely woven blend of stories, prayers and Scriptures that provide clarity and inspiration to see and do God's will.

My children and I are so grateful to the Lord for giving me the perfect wife and giving them the perfect mother for our family.

Just as she has put her heart into sharing this great tool with you, we pray you will put your heart into grasping the blessing that is wrapped in these pages.

May God bless and keep you!

--Derek Young

INTRODUCTION

Wesley L. Duewel, author of the book *Mighty Prevailing Prayer*, teaches very specifically that prevailing prayer "obtains the answers sought." *Divine Strategies for Life in Today's World* provides specific prayers and Scriptures for defined, everyday situations in business, parenthood, young adulthood and other life stages. Through prayer and "the sword of the spirit, which is the word of God" (Ephesians 6:17), believers can receive divine revelation for solving problems, overcoming fear, coping with grief, finding purpose in life, dealing with rejection, achieving success, increasing wealth, obtaining healing, building character, correcting vices, being led to repentance and much, much more.

The chapters in the book are categorized by specific life scenarios, prayers and Scriptures that address specific areas of focus.

EDITOR'S NOTE

Unless indicated otherwise, all Scripture quotations are from the New Revised Standard Version (1989), New York, N.Y.: Oxford University Press, Inc. Other passages are quoted from The Message: The Bible in Contemporary Language by Eugene H. Peterson (2005), Colorado Springs, Colo.: Nav Press.

CHAPTER 1

DIVINE STRATEGIES FOR LIFE IN TODAY'S WORLD

The presence of God, in and of itself, provides the optimal environment for a conversation with Him. God, the father, delights in sharing and interacting with His children in rich fellowship that honors and acknowledges His glory, majesty and power. Sometimes in life, believers can receive a divine revelation from the still, small voice of God that provides guidance in the most impossible circumstances. In the secret place, believers can receive a word from God and, in unimaginable ways, experience peace in the middle of the storm.

Savor the divine prayer strategies presented in this chapter. Use your prayer journal to add your own life scenarios, specific prayers and Scriptures. Document God's answers to create a memorial of stones that mark your passage over the Jordan Rivers of life.

CHAPTER 1-1

Divine Strategies:
Prayer and the Word of God

Daily, believers are bombarded with negative images, messages, temptations and behavior from so-called "friends." We often feel challenged in making positive, effective decisions in responding and reacting to these negative influences. Often, fear and anger may motivate believers to want to choose negative, emotionally charged strategies in handling daily challenges. However, God wants us to choose divine strategies such as kindness toward others, discernment in selecting friends, good stewardship in using money, cooperation with appropriate authority figures, wisdom in using words and courage to walk alone. Above all, God wants believers to use the power of prayer as the enabling force behind each divine strategy.

Christian parents can equip children to live well and to overcome obstacles by teaching them to use prayer as a strategy in dealing with issues they face. We can teach them, "For mortals it is impossible, but for God all things are possible" (Matthew 19:26b, NRSV). We can tell them, "The prayer of the righteous is powerful and effective" (James 5:16b, NRSV). We can meet and overcome challenges through prayer, which should include thanks and praise to God, petition or prayer requests, Scripture promises and faith to believe the solution will come.

DIVINE STRATEGY

Prayer Focus: Loving God, help my children and me to come to know you. Thank you for the beauty of relationship and connectivity through the power of prayer and your holy Word. Help us to know that wherever we are and whatever we face, prayer is always available, and that you answer prayer by giving us divine strategies that will work for us in our daily lives. Amen.

Scripture Focus — Luke 11:1-13, NRSV: Jesus "was praying in a certain place, and after he had finished, one of his disciples said to him, 'Lord, teach us to pray, as John taught his disciples.'"

REFLECTION

_____
_____
_____
_____
_____
_____
_____
_____
_____
_____
_____
_____
_____
_____
_____
_____
_____
_____
_____
_____
_____
_____

CHAPTER 1-2

A Word from the Lord

Anyone who is fired from a job, especially unjustly, knows how it feels to be afraid. Fear of not finding another job before losing assets, health or personal possessions may begin to cloud the mind. Fear that before finding work, savings will be exhausted, is terrifying. Fear of being unable to care properly for dependent family members can be gripping. Fear of losing friends, because of the eventual inability to maintain one's social standing, can arise and nearly overtake emotional well-being. The thoughts and fears of the unknown and the loss of self-esteem catapult even "the believer" into a place that seems like a wilderness. The inevitable question becomes, "God, what shall I do?"

Sometimes, in every believer's life, he or she does not know what to do. The dilemma can be caused by job loss, death or disability of a loved one, problems with children of any age, betrayal, divorce and health issues. The list goes on and on. To the believer who faces any of these dilemmas, there is good news! God has the solution to all problems!

Recently, I had the opportunity to minister as a background singer for a gospel artist. One of the songs through which we minister is Thomas Whitfield's, "We Need a Word from the Lord." The timely words herald the message:

"We don't need another political uprising,
We don't need another conqueror on the scene.
What we need is a special word,
that will burn within our hearts
and give us direction from above.

Chorus:
We need a word from the Lord,
a word from the Lord,

Just one word from the Lord,
will move all the doubts
and cause the sun to shine,
and give peace of mind;
speak Lord, speak."

The Bible says, "If any of you is lacking in wisdom, ask God, who gives to all generously and ungrudgingly, and it will be given you" (James 1:5, NRSV).

Perhaps one of the most beloved Scriptures is Luke 11:9-13, NRSV. "And I tell you, Ask, and it will be given you; seek, and you will find; knock, and it will be opened to you. For every one who asks receives, and the one who seeks finds, and to the one who knocks it will be opened. What mother or father among you, if a child asks for a fish, instead of a fish will give a serpent; or if a child asks for an egg, will give a scorpion? If you then, who are evil, know how to give good gifts to your children, how much more will God … give the Holy Spirit to those who ask?" Therefore, it's important for believers to pray and seek God's Word that provides the wisdom needed in every circumstance. Be assured that God will answer and enlighten in ways never imagined.

DIVINE STRATEGY

Prayer Focus: Loving God, today my circumstances seem insurmountable. I must make decisions, and as I search my mind, clear answers are not there. I know you not only have solutions I can use, but you also have the grace I need to believe you will work it out for me as only you can. I thank you, God, and I praise you, right now, because I know it is already done in Jesus' name! Amen.

Scripture Focus — Proverbs 3:5-6a, The Message: "Trust God from the bottom of your heart; don't try to figure out everything on your own. Listen for God's voice in everything you do, everywhere you go."

REFLECTION

_____
_____
_____
_____
_____
_____
_____
_____
_____
_____
_____
_____
_____
_____
_____
_____
_____
_____
_____
_____

CHAPTER 1-3

Peace in the Middle of a Storm

One of my favorite hymns is "Master, the Tempest Is Raging" written by Mary A. Baker. The song was inspired by the beloved biblical account of Jesus and the disciples at sea when a strong storm arises and threatens to demolish the boat with them in it. Awestruck, the disciples wake Jesus and say, "Lord, save us! We are perishing!" (Matthew 8:25, NRSV). Jesus admonishes them for their lack of faith and then commands the wind and the waves to be still.

This poignant text demonstrates to believers that in life, we will experience frightening situations that may cause us to feel hopeless and helpless. We may even be afraid of the threatening circumstances because of the magnitude of the problem. Yet, we can be assured that when we access the person of Jesus Christ internally through the Holy Spirit, we can have peace in the storm. As Christians, we have the same power to speak to winds and waves all around us, tossing and driving us, and command them to be still.

Be comforted by these words:

"Master, the tempest is raging!
The billows are tossing high!
The sky is o'er shadowed with blackness,
No shelter or help is nigh;
Carest Thou not that we perish?
How canst Thou lie asleep,
When each moment so madly is threat'ning
A grave in the angry deep?

Refrain:
The winds and the waves shall obey Thy will,
Peace, be still! Whether the wrath of the storm-tossed sea
Or demons, or men, or whatever it be.
No water can swallow the ship where lies
The Master of ocean, and earth, and skies;
They shall sweetly obey Thy will,
Peace, be still! Peace, be still!
They all shall sweetly obey Thy will,
Peace, peace, be still."

DIVINE STRATEGY

Prayer Focus: Loving God, I pray for peace in the middle of my storm, knowing that at the name of Jesus, every knee bows and every demon trembles. Help me to speak to my circumstances and command your peace. Amen.

Scripture Focus — Philippians 4:6, NRSV: "Do not worry about anything, but in everything by prayer and supplication with thanksgiving let your requests be made known to God. And the peace of God, which surpasses all understanding, will guard your hearts and your minds in Christ Jesus."

REFLECTION

_____

_____

_____

_____

_____

_____

_____

_____

_____

_____

_____

_____

_____

_____

_____

_____

_____

_____

_____

_____

CHAPTER 1 - 4

The Secret Place

The Secret Garden, a children's classic novel, by Frances Hodgson Burnett, is my favorite book of all time. While studying in school, doing homework or playing, I could not wait to get back to reading this fascinating story about a young British girl, Mary Lennox, who grows bitter and mean-spirited when her wealthy parents, too selfish to raise and care for her, often leave her to be reared by the family servants. When a plague of cholera kills her parents and the servants, Mary is sent to live with an uncle. She discovers a secret garden that changes her life and mends her heart.

Sometimes in life, people, places and circumstances create bitterness and walls of distrust, anger and resentment in our hearts. Our experiences may cause us to fear and to react defensively at all times, because we are afraid. God assures us of a secret place where we can go and not only reveal our true selves, but also receive healing and restoration for our souls. The Psalmist, David, writes in Psalm 91:1-2, NRSV, "You who live in the shadow of the Most High, who abide in the shadow of the Almighty, will say to the Lord, 'My refuge and my fortress; my God, in whom I trust."

Like Mary Lennox from *The Secret Garden*, we too can go to a secret place in God and find solace, truth, wisdom, help in the time of trouble, unconditional love, forgiveness, joy and empowerment to go back into the world, filled with peace and contentment despite our circumstances. Because God loves us, God will deliver us and set us on high. God knows our names. When we pray, God will answer in time of trouble. God will deliver and honor us. With long life, God will satisfy us and show us salvation.

DIVINE STRATEGY

Prayer Focus: Loving God, thank you for being my secret place, my rock and my salvation. Remind me that I can be all that I am before you and still be accepted and loved. Thank you always for "having my back" so I can relax and live confidently. I know you understand what concerns me and assure me that this, too, shall pass. Amen.

Scripture Focus — Psalm 27:5, NRSV: "For [God] will hide me in his shelter in the day of trouble; he will conceal me under the cover of his tent; he will set me high on a rock."

REFLECTION

_____

_____

_____

_____

_____

_____

_____

_____

_____

_____

_____

_____

_____

_____

_____

_____

_____

_____

_____

_____

CHAPTER 1-5

The Power of Fellowship

For humans, social competence is of utmost importance. The ability to make friends, relate in marriage, belong to active groups and organizations and influence others is essential to our well-being. We feel fellowship when we share mutual interests, experiences and activities.

In 2012, my family joined several other families on a trip to Henning, Tenn., to visit the home of Alex Haley, renowned author of the book, *Roots*. During our time together, we enjoyed the kind of fellowship that creates ties that bind. The group was large enough to warrant the trip, but small enough to make real connections. We spent time sharing mutual interests, experiences, and activities, and having rich conversations. I think we all came away feeling a little closer to one another.

Fellowship with God works exactly the same way. It is achieved in time spent sharing mutual interests, experiences and activities because God is a Spirit, with a personality or personhood in addition to omniscience and omnipresence. Communing with God requires becoming aware of God's presence in our lives. When we spend time in fellowship with God, we grow closer to one another. We learn God's character, which fosters our respect and care for God. When we read or listen to God's Word through past and present prophets, we deepen our fellowship and add to the richness of the relationship over time.

"If we claim that we experience a shared life with [God] and continue to stumble around in the dark, we're obviously lying through our teeth — we're not living what we claim. But if we walk in the light, God ... being the light, we also experience a shared life with one another." (1 John 1:6-7a, The Message)

One of the most important by-products of fellowship with God is living according to the principles God espouses. Jesus proclaimed that he and God are one. "Whoever has seen me has seen the Father" (John 14:9b, NRSV). Therefore, fellowship with God is also evidenced by becoming like God. As we become aware of God's presence in our lives; share our interests, activities and desires; listen to God's interests and desires; and notice God's works, we strengthen and deepen our relationship with God. God then comes to trust us as we learn to trust God. Together, through the power of fellowship, God can move through us in the world.

DIVINE STRATEGY

Prayer Focus: Loving God, I want to focus on you and spend time sharing mutual interests, activities, desires and experiences to strengthen and take our fellowship to a deeper level. Help me recognize your presence in my life and appreciate getting to know you. Amen.

Scripture Focus — James 4:8a, NRSV: "Draw near to God, and he will draw near to you."

REFLECTION

_____

_____

_____

_____

_____

_____

_____

_____

_____

_____

_____

_____

_____

_____

_____

_____

_____

_____

_____

_____

_____

_____

_____

CHAPTER 2

DIVINE STRATEGIES FOR THE MIND, SOUL AND BODY

Everyday life can try the patience and the virtue of even the most committed and mature believers. God's grace is available to increase the capacity for love, forgiveness, long-suffering and other fruits of the Spirit.

The divine strategic prayers and Scriptures presented in the life scenarios in this chapter target specific areas in the believer's life that are usually the most difficult to master: taming the tongue, not taking offense and maintaining the body, the temple of the Holy Spirit.

Take the time to study the prayer strategies in this chapter and gain a full understanding and revelation for how to choose the more excellent way.

CHAPTER 2-6

Watch Your Words

"This is a talking world," my father used to say. Daily, copious news stories, reality TV shows and "tell-all" talk shows bombard us. It seems everyone has something to say, and often the words are harsh and biting. People settle disputes with words that wound. Spouses criticize each other with hurtful words. Children bully other children with words that cut so deep, they cause irreparable emotional damage or even death. Friends gossip and reveal confidences that ruin relationships forever. Employees lose jobs due to insubordinate and disrespectful speech.

We can find many specific instructions for how we as Christians are to use our tongues. Perhaps the most important Scriptural declaration to remember is Proverbs 18:21, NRSV: "Death and life are in the power of the tongue; and those who love it will eat its fruits". Every day, believers have the opportunity to shape their lives and the lives of others with words. Though we sometimes must use words to warn and discipline others, believers should primarily use words to instruct, praise and affirm. We must carefully choose words that speak life into family, friends and co-workers and cause them to flourish in every circumstance.

DIVINE STRATEGY

Prayer Focus: Loving God, cause me to be ever mindful that words affect souls. Help me to remember I am accountable to you for using my words to heal and not hurt; to warn and not wound; to praise and not plot; and to speak life and not death. Amen.

Scripture Focus — Ephesians 4:29, NRSV: "Let no evil talk come out of your mouths, but only what is useful for building up, as there is need, so that your words may give grace to those who hear."

REFLECTION

_____
_____
_____
_____
_____
_____
_____
_____
_____
_____
_____
_____
_____
_____
_____
_____
_____
_____
_____
_____
_____
_____

Guard Your Heart

For the past 10 years, the American Heart Association has used the "Go Red" message and brand to raise attention and awareness to heart disease as the leading cause of death in women. Millions of women's groups and organizations have rallied to march, influence health-policy changes, encourage more research and raise funds to help women become more intentional about preventing heart disease. Workshops and weight-loss programs geared toward empowering women to be proactive about heart health abound.

God cares about believers' hearts as well. God cares especially about the emotional component of our psyche, which has also become known as the "heart." It is the place from which the energy and vitality for optimal functioning flows so we can multitask — work, care for our loved ones, create and maintain friendships, and pray to a loving God.

Proverbs 4:23, NRSV, encourages, "Keep your heart with all vigilance, for from it flow the springs of life." It is so important for us to evaluate situations and circumstances carefully and discern the best action to take. The connection between the physical heart and the emotional heart is very strong. In fact, our emotional heart can positively or adversely affect the function of the physical heart. Thoughts, stress levels, rehearsed conversations and encounters, relationship issues, anxieties about children and fears about health all contribute to the health of our physical heart.

In his letter to the Philippians (4:8-9, NRSV), the apostle Paul teaches strategies for guarding the heart. "Finally, beloved, whatever is true, whatever is honorable, whatever is just, whatever is pure, whatever is pleasing, whatever is commendable, if there is any excellence and if there is anything worthy of praise, think about these things. Keep on doing the things that you have learned and received and heard and seen in me, and the God of peace will be with you."

Believers must commit to studying and using biblical strategies for guarding the heart with all diligence to fulfill God's purpose and finish the work assigned on earth.

DIVINE STRATEGY

Prayer Focus: God, grant me the serenity to accept the things I cannot change; the courage to change the things I can; and the wisdom to know the difference. Amen.

--The Serenity Prayer, Reinhold Niebuhr

Scripture Focus — Proverbs 17:22, NRSV: "A cheerful heart is a good medicine, but a downcast spirit dries up the bones."

REFLECTION

_____

_____

_____

_____

_____

_____

_____

_____

_____

_____

_____

_____

_____

_____

_____

_____

_____

_____

_____

_____

_____

_____

_____

CHAPTER 2-8

Don't Take Offense

In a fallen world, it is impossible to get through life without experiencing negative words and actions from others. Jealousy, anger, bitterness, resentment, misunderstanding and mean-spiritedness are among the myriad of motives for offending. Perhaps the most difficult emotional response to quell is the feeling of being offended. It happens so quickly and wounds so effectively that, often, one doesn't take the time to employ rational thinking. However, it is important and necessary to acquire the discipline, emotional intelligence and spiritual capacity to refuse to take offense. That's right; offense is something people give that others can refuse to take.

The Bible gives clear instruction for how to handle offense. "Those with good sense are slow to anger, and it is their glory to overlook an offense" (Proverbs 19:11, NRSV). Of all the Scriptures that address dealing with offense, this verse is the most succinct and explanatory. It is wise to overlook an offense. We produce patience when we overlook an offense, and doing so contributes to one's glory or character. Being offended causes sin because the reaction to an offense is often retaliatory. The person offended feels justified in lashing out at the offender. Hurt feelings or bruised egos can cause a domino effect of continually hurled offenses.

Offenses given by close friends or family can trigger the greatest emotional response. A desire to be well regarded and respected can make us take offense. Sometimes, children can cause parents to feel offended and take offense. With hurtful words and actions, bosses, coworkers, spouses, siblings and pastors can touch places in the heart that pierce like daggers. But, if believers refuse to take the offense by deflecting the fiery darts with the shield of faith, we hinder the daggers from penetrating, and no injury occurs. Without hurt, there is usually no reaction. So, let us endeavor to refuse to take offense by applying this simple formula. When an offense is given, advises author Kate McVeigh, "Don't nurse it. Don't rehearse it. Just disperse it and God will reverse it."

DIVINE STRATEGY

Prayer Focus: Loving God, help me to refuse to accept offense by knowing who I am in you. Increase my capacity to show patience and wisdom and to deflect offenses with the shield of faith. Amen.

Scripture Focus — Matthew 24:10, NRSV: "Then many will fall away, and they will betray one another and hate one another."

REFLECTION

_____
_____
_____
_____
_____
_____
_____
_____
_____
_____
_____
_____
_____
_____
_____
_____
_____
_____
_____
_____
_____
_____
_____

CHAPTER 2-9

Our Bodies, God's Temple

Everywhere you turn or look, you see an advertisement for a diet plan or pill, weight loss, liposuction, or fat-burning workout. You name it, and you'll find a fast fad for battling the bulge. With aging, many symptoms emerge. Losing weight can seem nearly impossible, no matter how many days of working out or low-calorie eating you may do.

It is important to be aware that the body is essential for fulfilling God's call on the life of the believer. Bodies are used in many ways throughout life, and we must care for them with diligence. With wisdom and understanding, believers also must study and learn how various foods affect the body. Choosing an internist who will not only provide excellent care, but who also will listen and be attuned to our holistic care needs is essential to maintaining health during the aging process.

Consider the Scripture, "Or do you not know that your body is a temple of the Holy Spirit within you, which you have from God, and that you are not your own? For you were bought with a price; therefore glorify God in your body" (1 Corinthians 6:19-20, NRSV). What does it mean to honor God with our bodies? I believe it means to maintain the mind and brain by thinking good thoughts. Maintain the soul and heart by speaking kind and positive words of affirmation. Maintain the physical body by eating food that nourishes the cells and keeps the complex interdependent physiological systems functioning properly. Maintain appearance with good grooming and hygiene practices. Most of all, maintain and increase spiritual development through prayer and meditation in order to receive instruction about how God wants to use our bodies to fulfill his reign on earth.

DIVINE STRATEGY

Prayer Focus: Loving God, give me your divine revelation and understanding about my body as a temple where the Holy Spirit resides. Help me to live in a way that respects and honors you in all I say and do. Teach me to love my body and appreciate its unique design for the purposes for which you intended. Amen.

Scripture Focus — Proverbs 31:30, NRSV: "Charm is deceitful, and beauty is vain, but a woman who fears the Lord is to be praised."

REFLECTION

_____

_____

_____

_____

_____

_____

_____

_____

_____

_____

_____

_____

_____

_____

_____

_____

_____

_____

_____

_____

_____

_____

You Get What You Say

Remember the beloved children's story, *The Little Engine That Could*? The author, Watty Piper, personifies a railroad engine hired to work in a station yard. When a large engine is asked to carry a long line of freight trains over a hill, the large engine refuses and tells the freight trains that it can't pull them because of the weight and the effort required. After several engines refuse, a smaller engine is asked to try, and this engine accepts the challenge. With mental fortitude, determination and the constant proclamation, "I think I can," the little engine does what engines with greater capacity do not believe they can do.

This deeply moving, yet very brief, story is a stark reminder that success begins in the mind, passes through the mouth in the form of spoken words and results in activity that produces the desired goal. Long before the story of *The Little Engine That Could*, ancient Scripture taught many lessons.

- "For just as the body without the spirit is dead, so faith without works is dead." (James 2:26, NRSV)
- "Now faith is the assurance of things hoped for, the conviction of things not seen." (Hebrews 11:1, NRSV)
- "If you have faith the size of a mustard seed, you will say to this mountain, 'Move from here to there,' and it will move; and nothing will be impossible for you." (Matthew 17:20b, NRSV)
- "You reap whatever you sow." (Galatians 6:7b, NRSV)
- "Those who bring thanksgiving as their sacrifice honor me; to those who go the right way I will show the salvation of God." (Psalm 50:23, NRSV)
- "From the fruit of the mouth, one's stomach is satisfied; the yield of the lips brings satisfaction. Death and life are in the power of the tongue, and those who love it will eat its fruits." (Proverbs 18:20-21, NRSV)

- "As it is written, 'I have made you the father of many nations' — in the presence of the God in whom he believed, who gives life to the dead and calls into existence the things that do not exist." (Romans 4:17, NRSV)

- "You brood of vipers! How can you speak good things, when you are evil? For out of the abundance of the heart the mouth speaks. The good person brings good things out of a good treasure, and the evil person brings evil things out of an evil treasure. I tell you, on the day of judgment you will have to give an account for every careless word you utter; for by your words you will be justified, and by your words you will be condemned." (Matthew 12:34-37, NRSV)

These Scriptural truths abound. Therefore, it is important to take the time to search for Scriptures that concur with positive proclamations. Recite them every day, and like the little engine that could, you may be surprised at how much you can do, just because you think and say you can.

DIVINE STRATEGY

Prayer Focus: Loving God, help me learn from the little engine that could and believe that no matter the situation, I can do what it takes to handle it. With you, I can pull the weight of life over the hills and mountains of obstacles and make it to my destination. Amen.

Scripture Focus — Philippians 4:13, The Message: "Whatever I have, wherever I am, I can make it through anything in the One who makes me who I am."

REFLECTION

_____
_____
_____
_____
_____
_____
_____
_____
_____
_____
_____
_____
_____
_____
_____
_____
_____
_____
_____
_____
_____
_____
_____

CHAPTER 3

DIVINE REVELATION OF THE PERSON OF JESUS CHRIST

The Son of God, who is God incarnate, came to the world as the ultimate ransom for the sins of the world and to create the opportunity for redemption and complete reconciliation, with God, after the fall of humanity. Acceptance of Christ and a commitment to be conformed to his image and likeness are the roles of the believer throughout life.

Therefore, one of God's divine strategies is to reveal the person of Jesus Christ to us. Remember Matthew 16:15-16, NRSV: "He said to them, 'But who do you say that I am?' Simon Peter answered, 'You are the Messiah, the Son of the living God.'"

In this chapter, spend time contemplating the magnitude of Christ's coming to save the world and bringing joy. Gain a rich understanding of how Jesus loves and how his example of love is a model for how believers should love.

CHAPTER 3-11

Joy to the World

Many years ago while browsing the bookstore, one of my favorite pastimes as a young adult, I was drawn to *Joy That Lasts* by Gary Smalley and Al Janssen. I can remember seeking God for answers in how to maintain peace and contentment in a world focused on riches and hedonistic pleasures. I was always thinking that, if only I were married with a family, I would be totally happy. In the book, the authors identify four areas in which most people seek joy: people, places, positions and possessions. As I pondered the truth of this insight, I realized we are actually taught to seek joy in these areas. We learn, consciously or subconsciously, that certain relationships will make us happy. We believe that only in specific places can we truly be content. We strive for positions in order to validate our self-worth, and we definitely place high value in what we own and can access.

The more I read, the more I resonated with the wisdom of these revelations. The more I could see that the "joy" produced in people, places, positions and possessions is only temporary at best and provides a false sense of security. When I arrived at what the writers call "finding the well that never runs dry," I was so enriched and enlightened to learn that only Jesus could create in me the kind of fulfillment that lasts for an eternity.

The Gospel according to John recounts the story of a Samaritan woman whom Jesus encounters at Jacob's Well as he and his disciples travel from Jerusalem to Galilee and stop at a village of Sychar to buy food and get water. The woman is at the well to draw water. Jesus interacts with her and asks her for water, even though it is not customary for Jews to interact with Samarians. He also recognizes her "thirst" and begins to tell her about her life though he is a stranger to her. He reveals that she continues to seek love, joy, peace, contentment and fulfillment in a host of broken, extramarital relationships. He promises to give her living water that will quench the thirst in her soul.

During special times like the Christmas season, believers must settle down long enough not only to celebrate Jesus' birth, but also to meet him at the "well" and allow him to give us the living water we need to bring us lasting joy. Take the time to focus on Jesus, not the cares and worries of the moment. Go back and read John 4:1-40 and experience this story and draw from its truth. You may be surprised at how quickly you will gain the peace that surpasses all understanding.

DIVINE STRATEGY

Prayer Focus: Loving God, I come to you just as I am, thankful that only you can give me lasting joy and satisfy my thirst. Meet me here, just as you met the Samaritan woman, and give me living water. Amen.

Scripture Focus — John 7:38, NRSV: "And let the one who believes in me drink. As the scripture has said, 'Out of the believer's heart shall flow rivers of living water.'"

REFLECTION

_____
_____
_____
_____
_____
_____
_____
_____
_____
_____
_____
_____
_____
_____
_____
_____
_____
_____
_____
_____
_____
_____

CHAPTER 3-12

Christ the Savior Is Born

Millions of parents all over the world experience the joy and wonder in the birth of a child. They look forward in anxious anticipation to the arrival of the expected boy or girl as they plan for several months for the long-awaited appearance of this new life.

During Advent and Christmas, Christians celebrate the birth of Jesus Christ that happened more than 2,000 years ago. Christ's birth was fraught with controversy. His mother was an engaged virgin whose confused husband-to-be wanted to put her away privately because of her pregnancy, rather than have her stoned, according to the custom of that day for this kind of circumstance. Caesar Augustus had issued a decree for all of the citizens to be taxed and to go their hometowns for taxation. An angel appeared to Joseph and explained that Mary was impregnated by the Holy Spirit and that she was to give birth to a Savior, Jesus, which means "God with us."

Mary and Joseph arrived in Bethlehem only to be told that the inns were full. The only place the expectant mother could possibly give birth was in a nearby stable. Humbly, Joseph and Mary went to the stable, and Mary gave birth to Jesus in a manger or feeding trough filled with hay for animals. The Nativity scene is the most anointed visual of a birth experience ever documented. The Gospel of Luke (2:7-11, NRSV) tells the story. "And she gave birth to her firstborn son, wrapped him in bands of cloth, and laid him in a manger, because there was no place for them in the inn. In that region there were shepherds living in the fields, keeping watch over their flock by night. Then an angel of the Lord stood before them, and the glory of the Lord shone around them, and they were terrified. But the angel said to them, 'Do not be afraid; for see — I am bringing you good news of great joy for all the people: to you is born this day in the city of David a Savior, who is the Messiah, the Lord.'"

On Christmas day, start a tradition of reading the story of Jesus' birth to your family. Share the grace afforded to us all by Christ's coming to earth in human form to demonstrate his ability to relate with all forms of human suffering and to empower us to be victorious over every challenge. As the joyous carol "O Come, All Ye Faithful" suggests, "O come, let us adore him, Christ the Lord"!

DIVINE STRATEGY

Prayer Focus: Loving God, we celebrate Jesus' birth and appreciate the splendor and majesty of Christ's humility in being born in a lowly manger. We remember the reason for the season and focus on thanksgiving. Amen.

Scripture Focus—Luke 2:13-14, NRSV: "And suddenly there was with the angel a multitude of the heavenly host, praising God and saying, 'Glory to God in the highest heaven, and on earth peace among those whom he favors!'"

REFLECTION

CHAPTER 3-13

Jesus Loves All

Multiculturalism, diversity and inclusion have become "buzzwords" in modern times to signify the raised consciousness of the most sophisticated people and organizations. The assumption is that those who use these words have a keen understanding of the concepts at the core, and that individuals have embraced these concepts complete with their nuances and far-reaching implications. Yet, while modern businesses and savvy society intelligentsia have welcomed multiculturalism, diversity and inclusion, sometimes we as Christians lag far behind in our willingness to appreciate differences.

Jesus himself, however, in his final words to his disciples, commissions them, "To go therefore and make disciples of all nations" (Matthew 28:19a, NRSV). The apostle Paul explains, in the famous "love chapter," 1 Corinthians 13, that love is the only lasting, effective virtue for dealing with people. Therefore, Christ expects his disciples to combine love, power and authority to seek and save the lost all over the world and to follow his example of accepting people as a precursor to teaching them—just as he communed with tax collectors, publicans, prostitutes and the like.

In the Old Testament, God carefully designs the plan of salvation by weaving an intricate tapestry of diverse people and circumstances to illustrate the key components of the behaviors that ultimately would comprise the foundational tenants of the Christian lifestyle and prescribed ministry process. Perhaps one of the most renowned and beloved stories of trial and triumph is the account of Joseph, who, through his journey from the pit to the palace, provides a traceable profile and model for incorporating multiculturalism in ministry by demonstrating key characteristics.

Openness: Joseph quickly adjusts to his fate as a prisoner sold into slavery by his evil brothers and develops a strategy for surviving by being open and willing to learn and understand Potiphar and the Egyptian culture.

Acceptance: Joseph learns the customs and mores of the Egyptian culture and adapts. Most importantly, he demonstrates respect for the people and their ways.

Trust: Joseph not only gives honor; he also is honorable in the way he reveres authority figures, diligently learns and masters the language, and presents an excellent work ethic in all tasks he performed with a humble attitude that does not include murmuring and complaining.

Learning: Joseph is not haughty and condescending toward the Egyptians. He willingly and readily learns their culture and way of doing things, embraces the best parts and practices those standards.

Understanding: Joseph endeavors to understand all facets of life and the various institutions of the culture, which eventually equips him to lead a people to whom he is a foreigner.

Serving: Finally, Joseph decides to serve rather than to be served, despite the conditions into which his brothers thrust him.

These characteristics which Joseph so dutifully demonstrated, teach present-day Christians how to serve and how to embrace diversity. Jesus also infused these characteristics into his daily ministry and showed the disciples how to win souls by demonstrating these six characteristics.

Christians have the unique opportunity to follow Joseph's and Christ's examples, and most importantly, to teach children to do likewise. This world is filled with all kinds of people who are different in many ways. The ability to interact, relate and mine for the gold in a variety of people is a much sought after behavioral competency.

DIVINE STRATEGY

Prayer Focus: Loving God, you said in your word that of all the virtues, love is the greatest. Empower and strengthen me to demonstrate genuine love, acceptance, inclusion and appreciation of people and their differences, realizing our similarities truly connect us to you. Amen.

Scripture Focus — Revelation 7:9, NRSV: "After this I looked, and there was a great multitude that no one could count, from every nation, from all tribes and peoples and languages, standing before the throne and before the Lamb, robed in white, with palm branches in their hands."

REFLECTION

_____

_____

_____

_____

_____

_____

_____

_____

_____

_____

_____

_____

_____

_____

_____

_____

_____

_____

_____

CHAPTER 4

HONOR: A DIVINE STRATEGY FOR SUCCESS IN LIFE

Honor is a virtue that is almost becoming extinct, especially in today's world. Children dishonor parents. Employees dishonor employers. Husbands dishonor wives. Nations dishonor leaders. People dishonor each other. Yet, God uses honor as a divine strategy to develop the character of humility and reverence for the structure of authority God created to establish order in a fallen world.

Yes, we see many tragic examples of leaders who abuse people who try to honor them. These experiences can cause confusion and disillusionment about the truth of God's command to honor. However, it is important for the believer to realize God is honorable and God honors those who chose to honor as an act of obedience.

The divine prayer strategies in this chapter will help you gain new revelation about the power of honor.

CHAPTER 4-14

Pray for Our President and Leaders

The 44th President of the United States, Barack Obama, was inaugurated for a second term, January 21, 2013, in another historic, unprecedented moment in U.S. history. Thousands sojourned to the nation's capital for this hallmark event in which the first African-American President of the United States took the oath to serve this country as commander in chief. Not since the marches and the magnitude of the Civil Rights movement and the signing of the Emancipation Proclamation has an event been more pivotal. The U.S. presidency is the highest office of authority in the land, and as citizens of the United States, our respect for the office and the leader is required.

Authority is of the utmost importance to God. Through the structure and order of government, God can work most effectively in the world. Through leaders, God's intent at a minimum is to exact justice, establish various systems and care for the poor. As Christians, we have a responsibility in our behavior toward leaders that is specifically documented in Scripture.

In the Apostle Paul's letter to the Romans (13:1, NRSV), he teaches, "Let every person be subject to the governing authorities; for there is no authority except from God, and those authorities that exist have been instituted by God."

It is clear in these Scriptures that believers are to revere those in authority. It is also clear that we are to pray for our leaders as Paul taught in his first letter to Timothy (2:1-4, NRSV), "First of all, then, I urge that supplications, prayers, intercessions, and thanksgivings be made for everyone, for kings and all who are in high positions, so that we may lead a quiet and peaceable life in all godliness and dignity. This is right and is acceptable in the sight of God our Savior, who desires everyone to be saved and to come to the knowledge of the truth." Let us, therefore, pray for the President and all leaders who govern as a form of reverence to God and to the leaders.

DIVINE STRATEGY

Prayer Focus: Loving God, I pray for the President of United States. I pray that you will lead, guide and protect the President and all those in the cabinet and Congress who work together for this republic. I also pray for all leaders, that they may govern wisely and with the best interest of the people they lead. Amen.

Scripture Focus — Psalm 105:15, NRSV: "Do not touch my anointed ones; do my prophets no harm."

REFLECTION

_____

_____

_____

_____

_____

_____

_____

_____

_____

_____

_____

_____

_____

_____

_____

_____

_____

_____

_____

_____

_____

_____

_____

CHAPTER 4-15

Parents as Leaders

In today's world, so many parents are heartbroken about their relationships with their children. They often struggle with how best to handle their children's disrespect and apparent anger.

As I look back over my life, I often think about my relationship with my parents before they passed away, and I feel sad for parents who feel as if they are at the "end of their rope" in their efforts to build a strong relationship with their children.

A pastor of a church in St. Louis, MO, wrote a play called "The Denied Mother." Much like today's parents the Mother in the play struggled with life after her husband left her for another woman when their daughter was an infant. Despite her grief and shame, the mother lifted her head, trusted in God, continued working and provided for her daughter. The story depicts the daughter as ungrateful, unloving and ultimately degrading of her mother to the extent that her mother died of a broken heart. It was not until the end of her mother's funeral that the daughter resurfaced and ran through the church doors just long enough to request that she view her mother before burial, to pour out love, regret and gratitude for her mother's endless sacrifices. But, it was too late. The estranged daughter's mother was gone, and the relationship could never be regained.

Mother's Day and Father's Day are internationally recognized times for being very intentional about expressing heartfelt feelings of love and gratitude toward mothers and fathers. Children, grandchildren, godchildren, adopted children or "play" children present significant parents and parent figures in their lives with cards, flowers, gifts, trips, poems and special surprises. Yet, God commands believers to express honor, love and respect to parents daily. It is important and necessary for children to realize the worth and value of parents and to find ways to navigate through identity crises at any age in a way that leaves room in their behavior for love, respect and honor. As parents, we must foster love, respect and honor through rearing with wisdom and setting strong boundaries for our children. In Hebrews 12:11, NRSV, we read, "Now, discipline always seems painful rather than pleasant at the time, but later it yields the peaceful fruit of righteousness to those who have been trained by it." Mothers must trust and believe these words from Proverbs 22:6, NRSV, "Train children in the right way, and when old, they will not stray."

If I were to speak directly to the mother in the play while she was rearing her daughter, to myself and to mothers everywhere, I would remind us all of this comforting Scripture, "Can a woman forget her nursing child, or show no compassion for the child of her womb?" (Isaiah 49:15, NRSV). Just as you grieve for the love, honor, respect, safety and protection of the child of your womb, God cares and will never leave or forsake you as a mother.

God gives children as an inheritance and a reward for a mother's heart. Just remember to pray for your children and remember that God knows, sees and cares. Do not give in to fear and despair concerning your children and their decisions. Rather, trust that God will give you the grace to endure disappointment and dissipate the resentment you may feel toward your children because of their poor choices. God also will allow you to forgive your children's faults and celebrate their successes and positive qualities.

God will lead, guide and protect your heart, if you will give it to God, a mender of broken hearts.

DIVINE STRATEGY

Prayer Focus: Loving God, I love my children and thank you for them. When they are young and small, they are underfoot, where I can protect and nurture them. As they grow up and leave the nest to live their own lives, they are and will forever be on my heart. Help me to have the faith and trust to know you will not give me more than I can bear. You will give me the wisdom to get through the times when my children experience physical, mental, emotional and spiritual growing pains. Comfort me and strengthen my resolve to believe that everything will be all right. Amen.

Scripture Focus — Philippians 1:6, NRSV: "I am confident of this, that the one who began a good work among you will bring it to completion by the day of Jesus Christ."

REFLECTION

CHAPTER 4-16

The Power of Honor

My husband's grandmother lived to be 94. Words cannot express how grateful we all felt to have had her with us for so long. In reflecting on my favorite memories, I miss her never-ending kindness toward me. How, lovingly, she would call me, if she knew we were planning a trip to visit her in St. Louis, and ask me what dessert I wanted. She knew peach cobbler is my favorite dessert and oatmeal raisin is my favorite cookie. I don't remember a time she did not make both for me. When Derek and I got married, she made us a wedding-ring quilt. The beautiful quilt displays her handiwork, and I could feel the love in each stitch. Over the years, she and I shared laughs and teasing, meal recipes, and hopes and dreams. Most of all, we shared our appreciation for one another.

"Give people their flowers, while they are still alive" is one of my husband's favorite sayings. It is a mantra he truly lives by and has taught me to embrace. God has something to say about the importance of honor. "'Honor you father and mother' — this is the first commandment with a promise: 'so that it may be well with you and you may live long on the earth'" (Ephesians 6:2-3, NRSV).

It is so important to honor people with kind words, respectful actions and helpful deeds. We live in a world where honor is hardly spoken, let alone practiced. Children dishonor their parents with disobedience and rebellion. They dishonor their friends by setting bad examples and making reckless decisions without regard to how those decisions affect or could affect others around them. Spouses dishonor each other by neglecting their emotions or by breaking their vows. Employees dishonor employers by unethical practices or vice versa. The list of ways in which people dishonor others is endless. Yet, God cares about how we treat the elderly, the sick, the downtrodden and the lonely and how we treat our relationship with God.

Why is it important to honor one another before the funeral? It edifies and encourages, and it is a virtue. It is the epitome of good character. Honor is also a wisdom key that unlocks the door to opportunity, especially if we honor the right person at the right time.

So, we will pause and take the time to honor Gran's memory and reflect on how much we loved her. What comforts us the most is that we all took the time to honor her and let her know how we felt about her while she was alive to hear it!

As believers, we should demonstrate honor, so that our children know how it looks and understand the requirement. They should see us honoring our parents, pastors, leaders, teachers, employers and friends, and we should require that they model that behavior. If we find they are dishonoring, we should correct them and teach them the importance of honor.

DIVINE STRATEGY

Prayer Focus: Loving God, help me to slow the pace of a busy life long enough to honor those around me who truly make a difference in my life. Help me to teach my children how to honor people and sow good seed, so that it will come back to them in their lives. Amen.

Scripture Focus — Proverbs 18:12, NRSV: "Before destruction one's heart is haughty, but humility goes before honor."

REFLECTION

_____
_____
_____
_____
_____
_____
_____
_____
_____
_____
_____
_____
_____
_____
_____
_____
_____
_____
_____
_____
_____
_____
_____
_____

CHAPTER 5

DIVINE REFRESHING

There comes a time in every believer's life journey when God provides divine refreshing. A sense of lasting peace, joy and rest descends upon the believer after a time or travail in prayer, fasting and waiting upon God.

The divine prayer strategies in this chapter will help to prepare the believer for an encounter with God that will provide the calm assurance that God never leaves nor forsakes and God brings believers to green pastures, still waters and restoration of the soul.

Journal your encounters and interactions with God during these times. As you look back—once you have passed through your circumstances—see how God's grace refreshed you. Notice God's presence in every season of your life.

CHAPTER 5-17

The Seasons of Your Life

Do you ever think of how the four seasons — winter, spring, summer and autumn —are so unique and distinctive in their characteristics and functions? Winter is characterized by frigid, cold climate and barren trees. Spring brings the budding of new life after consistent rains. The summer heat definitely takes off the chill of winter and spring, and autumn samples the temperatures of all of the seasons as the falling leaves remind us that everything must change.

King Solomon, the presumed author of Ecclesiastes, one of the most provocative books in the Bible, talks about the seasons of life in the third chapter of his pensive musings. Masterfully, the author states that he had observed the various nuances and contradictions of life and realized what he determined to be immutable, predictable patterns that everyone experiences in the expanse of time. He observed, "For everything there is a season, and a time for every matter under heaven: a time to be born, and a time to die; a time to plant, and a time to pluck up what is planted; a time to kill, and a time to heal; a time to break down, and a time to build up; a time to weep, and a time to laugh; a time to mourn, and a time to dance; a time to throw away stones, and a time to gather stones together; a time to embrace, and a time to refrain from embracing; a time to seek, and a time to lose; a time to keep, and a time to throw away; a time to tear, and a time to sew; a time to keep silence, and a time to speak; a time to love, and a time to hate; a time for war, and a time for peace." (Ecclesiastes 3:1-8, NRSV)

King Solomon's wisdom teaches that the only thing that is constant is change and that we must learn to recognize and embrace the seasons of our lives. "Jesus Christ is the same yesterday and today and forever" (Hebrews 13:8, NRSV). Through the seasons of our lives, we can be assured that God will never leave or forsake us. God's promises are true. God will lead, guide and protect us in every season, if we trust in him.

Today, you may be experiencing a season of darkness. Know that the light is on its way. You may be in a time of famine in a particular area in your life. The feast is being prepared just for you. You may be enjoying the best time of your life. However, when the time comes that it seems as though the "bottom has fallen out," be assured that you will rise again. Whatever the season, know that, in the words of an old hymn, written by Jennie Wilson, crippled and wheelchair bound, in the late 1800s, "Time is filled with swift transition, Naught of earth unmoved can stand. Build your hopes on things eternal, Hold to God's unchanging hand."

DIVINE STRATEGY

Prayer Focus: Loving God, I pray for the strength to allow the Holy Spirit to carry me through all the seasons of my life and to know that whether times are good or bad, happy or sad, you are always there. Amen.

Scripture Focus — Ecclesiastes 3:11a, The Message: "True, God made everything beautiful in itself and in its time."

REFLECTION

_____
_____
_____
_____
_____
_____
_____
_____
_____
_____
_____
_____
_____
_____
_____
_____
_____
_____
_____
_____
_____
_____
_____
_____
_____

CHAPTER 5-18

The Beauty of Spring

Spring is one of my favorite times of year. The flowers bloom. The birds chirp. Spring rain brightens and turns the tree leaves a vibrant green. All of the newness of the season serves to bring promise and a renewed sense of well-being and hope for the future. This is a time of year when reflection will surely bring revelation because the changing weather will help to provide clarity of focus.

It will be important to use this time to concentrate on how your spirit is being impressed to make changes or improvements in your life or to reconsider decisions you have already made. Perhaps you will find new enlightenment not considered during the dark night of the soul.

The Scriptures are full of God's encouragement to use nature's example in daily living. Matthew 6:1-34 beautifully illustrates how God's care for nature would never supersede God's love and care for us. "Therefore, I tell you, do not worry about your life, what you will eat or what you will drink, or about your body, what you will wear. Is not life more than food, and the body more than clothing? Look at the birds of the air; they neither sow nor reap nor gather into barns, and yet your heavenly Father feeds them. Are you not of more value than they? And can any of you by worrying add a single hour to your span of life? And why do you worry about clothing? Consider the lilies of the field, how they grow; they neither toil nor spin, yet I tell you, even Solomon in all his glory was not clothed like one of these. But if God so clothes the grass of the field, which is alive today and tomorrow is thrown into the oven, will he not much more clothe you — you of little faith? Therefore, do not worry, saying, 'What will we eat?' or 'What will we drink?' or 'What will we wear?' ... But strive first for the kingdom of God and his righteousness, and all these things will be given to you as well. So do not worry about tomorrow, for tomorrow will bring worries of its own. Today's trouble is enough for today." (Matthew 6:25-34, NRSV)

The believer can be assured as you enjoy this spring season. Take the time to smell the flowers, the morning dew, crisp days and all of the sights and sounds of the season. God will take care of you, your family and all that concerns you. Just as God restores and renews the earth, God will refresh, renew and restore your soul.

DIVINE STRATEGY

Prayer Focus: Loving God, thank you for the springtime and all that it brings to remind me that you are sovereign. I declare your majesty as I consider all that your hands have made. My soul will cry out in wonder as I proclaim your excellent greatness. My God, how great you are! Amen.

Scripture Focus — Psalm 118:24, The Message: "This is the very day God acted — let's celebrate and be festive!"

REFLECTION

_____
_____
_____
_____
_____
_____
_____
_____
_____
_____
_____
_____
_____
_____
_____
_____
_____
_____
_____
_____
_____
_____
_____

CHAPTER 5-19

Ring out the Old, Ring in the New

Happy New Year! We live for it. We watch for it. We plan for it. We look forward to it. We resolve to make changes in it. Yes, the New Year brings the awesome opportunity to begin again. The concept of the New Year gives the illusion that we can leave the past behind and start over. We seem to believe old habits and ways of thinking can be transformed by the stroke of midnight at the end of a calendar year.

If only it were that simple. The truth is, change is much more complicated and difficult than a strongly spoken resolution to change. Yet, change begins with a dogged decision. However, some decisions to change can only become a reality with the help of God's strength. In Scripture, we are reminded that God's grace is sufficient because in our weakness, God is made strong. Jesus Christ tells us to exchange our heavy yoke for his easy one. Doubting Thomas understood his limitations in believing that Christ had risen. He asked for help for his unbelief, even though he was trying to believe the surreal occurrence. There comes a time in every Christian's life when we need the empowerment that only the Holy Spirit can give in order to make necessary changes. Forgiveness is one of those resolutions that often requires supernatural ability, especially when the offense has far-reaching effects in our lives. We can say we forgive, but we must release our souls, (mind, will, and emotions), to God to work in us the heart change needed to behave in a forgiving way and, in time, to forget the sting of the offense.

Whether believers need to lose weight, spend less money, manage time better or stop or start a certain behavior, it is important to realize we can ask God, through prayer and petition, for divine empowerment to carry out our resolutions, so that we actually make the changes over time rather than believe they can be done overnight.

DIVINE STRATEGY

Prayer Focus: Loving God, I stand on your promise that with you, all things are possible. I release my faith to believe you can enable me to do all I should do and stop doing all I should not do. Change my heart and my mind by creating in me a clean heart and renewing a right spirit within me to carry out your purpose and will in my life. Amen.

Scripture Focus — Ephesians 3:20, The Message: "God can do anything, you know — far more than you could ever imagine or guess or request in your wildest dreams! He does it not by pushing us around but by working within us, his Spirit deeply and gently within us."

REFLECTION

_____
_____
_____
_____
_____
_____
_____
_____
_____
_____
_____
_____
_____
_____
_____
_____
_____
_____
_____
_____
_____

CHAPTER 5-20

God's Grace Is Perfect

The world was intensely engaged in the Trayvon Martin case, and some were appalled by what seemed an unjust verdict for George Zimmerman. News commentators, well-known attorneys and everyday people all weighed in with views about several aspects of the case, from the skewed evidence and ill-prepared witnesses to the perplexing reasons jurors gave for concluding that Zimmerman was justified in accosting and murdering an unarmed teen. Like so many parents of young African-American boys, the verdict left me feeling forlorn and bereft.

As I pondered how to respond to the devastating news and its far-reaching implications, a single tear rolled down my face. The mere thought of either one of my innocent, fun-loving, small-framed boys being perceived as a threat to a man with a gun gripped me with overwhelming fear, and my heart ached for Trayvon's parents. Facebook posts were filled with expressions of utter disbelief and outraged cries for justice. My own emotions churned as I read many of them, until I bowed my head and prayed, "Lord, Lord, what can I say to the world about my feelings? What should I say? What would YOU say?"

At that very moment, I felt as though God lifted my head and looked into my eyes to locate the depths of my soul. My spirit was keenly impressed with God's precious message to me. "Daughter, I know the pain of losing a child. Jesus was my only begotten son, and he, too, was unjustly and inhumanely murdered. Yet, I suffered it to be so and even planned it that way to serve a larger purpose. Then, three days after his death and burial, I resurrected him and thus redeemed a lost and dying world." Instantly, the burden and the heaviness of the weight I was feeling subsided, and I was able to totally cast my cares upon a God who knows all, sees all, cares about all and has experienced the greatest of all human suffering, the loss of a child.

Throughout life, the believer will experience much loss, pain, sorrow and suffering. But God promises to give beauty for ashes and joy for mourning. God works everything together for good. Although Trayvon Martin, like countless children through the ages, has passed from time to eternity, God has a plan and a purpose for his untimely death, just as God had for Jesus' death. We can be assured that God's plan will bring about newness of life in the struggle for justice and equality, and as composer Charles Albert Tindley said, "We'll Understand It Better By and By."

DIVINE STRATEGY

Prayer Focus: Loving God, comfort the hearts of parents everywhere who have lost children. Help me to live in faith and not fear, that you, who have begun a good work in the lives of my children, will see it through to completion until the day of Jesus Christ, and to trust you for whatever that will look like. Amen.

Scripture Focus — 2 Corinthians 12:9b, NRSV: "My grace is sufficient for you, for my power is made perfect in weakness. So, I will boast all the more gladly of my weaknesses, so that the power of Christ may dwell in me."

REFLECTION

_____

_____

_____

_____

_____

_____

_____

_____

_____

_____

_____

_____

_____

_____

_____

_____

_____

_____

_____

_____

_____

_____

THE DIVINE CALL OF MOTHERHOOD

This chapter is specifically for mothers and women.

God has a special place in His heart for mothers. The call of motherhood requires additional support from a community of other women and groups. It is important for mothers to understand their roles as mothers, be mentored as mothers, develop friendships as mothers and maintain the heart of a mother for all children.

The divine prayer strategies and life scenarios in this chapter will help mothers gain the strength of mind and spirit needed to cope with the daily pressures of motherhood. Journaling your experience of God's divine guidance and protection for you as a mother will be a tremendous source of reassurance that God is always there and gives special grace to mothers.

CHAPTER 6-21

Godly Counsel for Mothers

Have you ever thought, "Wow, I wish I could just talk to an older, more experienced woman about certain topics I'm concerned about and get her wisdom? Surely, somewhere out there is a seasoned grandmotherly woman or even a jazzy senior who knows the ropes and can school me on how to get through these tough middle years"?

Maybe your mother has died or your relationship with your mother just doesn't lend itself to the kind of conversations you feel comfortable having with her. The Bible has something to say about younger women's relationships with older women and the importance of developing them. Older women in ancient days were admonished to teach young women how to love their husbands and children. These women had a significant role to play in the lives of the young women they mentored.

I reflected on an outstanding talk about parenting presented by a great woman who is a longtime leader and role model. In all the years I have seen and known her in professional circles, this was the first time I heard her speak about life at home. I was so moved by her many pearls of wisdom that I connected with her at the end of the conference and talked to her to learn more. In that brief exchange, I gained knowledge about some things to do for my children's development that I had not considered.

A couple of years ago, I had the great opportunity to "sit at the feet" of a phenomenal group of seasoned wives, mothers and professionals to gain their wisdom about living a successful life, maintaining good health and well-being and raising amazing children. The event was so powerful I thought we should convene these "fireside chats" on a regular basis. In considering the valuable information they shared, I encourage you to identify seasoned women and connect with them in a mentor/mentee relationship. You will be so enriched by the experience.

DIVINE STRATEGY

Prayer Focus: Loving God, you said in your Word that in a multitude of counsel, there is wisdom. In this year, guide me to a seasoned woman with whom I can share confidences, ask questions and receive godly direction and proven strategies for the various aspects of my life. Give me the humility and favor to interact with this woman and learn from her. Thank you in advance for using this relationship in my spiritual growth and development. Amen.

Scripture Focus — Titus 2:3-5, The Message: "Guide older women into lives of reverence so they end up as ... models of goodness. By looking at them, the younger women will know how to love their husbands and children, be virtuous and pure, keep a good house, be good wives. We don't want anyone looking down on God's Message because of their behavior."

REFLECTION

CHAPTER 6-22

A Mother's Reward

In today's world, many women may work outside of the home to provide for their families as single parent heads of their households, or they may work to help their spouses provide for the family. Many women, with or without families to support, may also work to earn income in professions that fulfill their vocations and express their gifts and talents as leaders, doctors, engineers, pastors etc. God blesses and works through career women to accomplish much good in the earth. Sometimes, stay-at-home moms may feel they pale in comparison to other women and/or mothers who are earning income and gaining recognition among their peers in jobs or careers.

Yet, among the many roles God called women to fulfill in ancient times and today, one of the roles for which God designed women physiologically, psychologically, and emotionally, is that of mother. "Don't you see that children are God's best gift? The fruit of the womb, his generous legacy? Like a warrior's fistful of arrows are the children of a vigorous youth. Oh, how blessed are you parents, with your quivers full of children! Your enemies don't stand a chance against you; you'll sweep them right off your doorstep." (Psalm 127:3-5, The Message)

God uses the womb of a woman and the marital union to bring forth godly seed. God then uses the population of godly people to reproduce his reign on earth and lighten a dark world.
A mother who has chosen to focus on her family should never diminish her position or feel slighted. Oftentimes, God even uses career setbacks, such as layoffs or terminations, as prime opportunities to help mothers reestablish or enhance their connection with their children or to equip them for life through increased spiritual development. Motherhood is a high calling. As William Ross Wallace wrote, "The Hand That Rocks the Cradle is the Hand that Rules the World."

DIVINE STRATEGY

Prayer Focus: Loving God, thank you for calling me to motherhood and rewarding me with children. Help me to be ever mindful that my role as mother is the highest calling. Give me the wisdom to know that as long as I have children, I can never retire, be laid off or terminated as mother. It is a God-given role I have been ordained to fulfill. Amen.

Scripture Focus — Proverbs 31:27-28, NRSV: "She looks well to the ways of her household, and does not eat the bread of idleness. Her children rise up and call her happy; her husband too, and he praises her."

REFLECTION

_____

_____

_____

_____

_____

_____

_____

_____

_____

_____

_____

_____

_____

_____

_____

_____

_____

_____

_____

_____

_____

CHAPTER 6-23

The Power of Friendship among Women

You may remember the childhood song, "Make new friends, but keep the old. One is silver, the other is gold." Friendship is an important and necessary component of social structure that extends beyond the family structure. It involves the process of meeting and choosing people with similar interests, beliefs, ideas, and personality traits—and sometimes even opposite personality traits—with whom to spend recreational time. The depth of friendships can vary from casual to close. Some friendships are deeper than family relationships or they can become equivalent to family relationships. Most of all, friendships are vital to well-being, especially for women.

In my daily work, I often hear women say they have more men friends than women friends or they get along better with men than they do other women. I have seen many friendships among women end tragically due to gossip, negative competition, jealousy, deceit, betrayal of confidences and the list goes on and on. Sadly, bitterness and resentment in friendships gone awry often causes irreparable damage, and the friendships are never restored.

God speaks clearly about friendships and gives specific instructions for successfully forming and managing them. "Some friends play at friendship, but a true friend sticks closer than any kin" (Proverbs 18:24, NRSV). "A friend loves at all times." (Proverbs 17:17a, NRSV). "No one has greater love than this, to lay down one's life for one's friends" (John 15:13, NRSV). God's Word tells us friends and friendships are to be handled with the utmost care and a friend possesses characteristics that will pass the test of time and circumstance. In other words, a friend is not "some-timey," a word we used "back in the day." Proverbs 6:16 (The Message) shares six things God hates and one more God loathes with a passion: "eyes that are arrogant, a tongue that lies, hands that murder the innocent, a heart that hatches evil plots, feet that race down a wicked track, a mouth that lies under oath, a troublemaker in the family."

What can happen when women form lasting friendships based on mutual respect, trust, courage, commitment and sacrifice? Marriages can survive. Children can have positive reinforcement of the values taught in the home. The collective enterprise of cooperative women can change the world.

DIVINE STRATEGY

Prayer Focus: Loving God, thank you for giving me the capacity to be a true friend and for giving me true friends. Help me to value all of my friendships and to treat other women as I would want to be treated. Help me to use my influence to help instead of harm. Help me to know that every woman is like a piece to a puzzle, tapestry or mosaic; she is unique and necessary for completion of the larger scheme. Therefore, I will help her find the place where she fits, and I will not seek to tear her down because I understand there is room for all of us. Amen.

Scripture Focus — Proverbs 12:26, NRSV: "The righteous gives good advice to friends, but the way of the wicked leads astray."

REFLECTION

_____

_____

_____

_____

_____

_____

_____

_____

_____

_____

_____

_____

_____

_____

_____

_____

_____

_____

_____

_____

CHAPTER 6-24

Hope for Mothers

Rearing children is one of the most challenging jobs on earth. As mothers, we are responsible for contributing greatly to the social, physiological, psychological and spiritual development of our children. Yet, no standard operating-procedures manual or instruction booklet tells mothers, step by step, everything to do to rear children successfully. Sure, we can find many books and seminars about parenting and well-documented insights into how to raise successful, positive, confident, contributing children. Yet, there is no "one size that fits all", so mothers do the best they can do.

The Holy Scriptures provide the assurance that "for mortals, it is impossible, but, for God all things are possible." (Matthew 19:26, NRSV). The Bible offers wisdom. "Train children in the right way, and when old, they will not stray" (Proverbs 22:6, NRSV). "If any of you is lacking in wisdom, ask God, who gives to all generously and ungrudgingly, and it will be given you" (James 1:5, NRSV). Jesus left us with another comforter, the Holy Spirit, to guide mothers into all truth. I am convinced that through the Bible, God wanted to give mothers just enough of the basic steps and guidelines for childrearing that we would lean on God as our divine teacher and mentor as we parent. God promises never to leave or forsake any believer, especially mothers and parents.

So, mothers, rise up today with confidence, knowing that God entrusted you with your children, for they are your reward. Realize that God believes in you. God will coach you and give you strategies to defeat the enemy. If you feel challenged, and maybe even somewhat defeated, take time to come off the court or the field and huddle with God, your parent; Jesus, your personal trainer; and the Holy Spirit, your counselor. Allow them give you some "plays" that will change the course, flip the script and help you navigate through the murky waters of uncertainty you may be facing right now in rearing your children. Believe that you are more than a conqueror through God who loves you. Most of all, remember your faith will give you the victory to overcome.

DIVINE STRATEGY

Prayer Focus: Loving God, give me the wisdom I need as a mother to bring out the God-given purpose and gifts you have bestowed upon my children. Help me to lead, guide, protect and love them in ways that inspire them to greatness. Please, heal my children in every area where they may be weak and help them to become strong in Jesus' name. Amen.

Scripture Focus—Proverbs 31:26, NRSV: "She opens her mouth with wisdom, and the teaching of kindness is on her tongue."

REFLECTION

_____
_____
_____
_____
_____
_____
_____
_____
_____
_____
_____
_____
_____
_____
_____
_____
_____
_____
_____
_____
_____

CHAPTER 7

WALKING IN DIVINE NATURE

In Matthew 5:17, NRSV, Jesus said, "Do not think that I have come to abolish the law or the prophets; I have come not to abolish but to fulfill." He taught that the Ten Commandments can be summed up into two: "You shall love the Lord your God with all your heart, and with all your soul, and with all your mind" and "You shall love your neighbor as yourself." Therefore, the believer's purpose in life can be summed up as loving God, loving others and loving self.

The divine strategies in this chapter speak to the activities of love on a daily basis. Allow the life scenarios, prayers and Scriptures to challenge you to think about what you do intentionally to show love to others. Journal your experiences and see how God uses you to do great things on earth in ways you may never have imagined.

CHAPTER 7-25

The Power of Spiritual Maturity

From the moment most parents learn they are expecting a child, they begin to think and dream about what they will do to help their child mature emotionally as the child grows physically. Good parents want to support the stages of development with patience for the child's youth and inexperience, yet introduce safe learning opportunities to strengthen his or her decision making. Parents want to contribute all they can to the process of producing a self-managed adult.

The apostle Paul presents a balanced perspective on God's highest standard of spiritual maturity in his great first epistle to the church at Corinth, commonly known as the "love chapter." Like earthly parents, God designed a program to help God's children mature spiritually. Love is the pinnacle of behavior God requires Christians to demonstrate as evidence of spiritual maturity. Paul explains love to the church at Corinth as follows:

"If I speak in the tongues of mortals and of angels, but do not have love, I am a noisy gong or a clanging cymbal. And if I have prophetic powers, and understand all mysteries and all knowledge, and if I have all faith, so as to remove mountains, but do not have love, I am nothing. If I give away all my possessions, and if I hand over my body so that I may boast, but do not have love, I gain nothing. Love is patient; love is kind; love is not envious or boastful or arrogant or rude. It does not insist on its own way; it is not irritable or resentful; it does not rejoice in wrongdoing, but rejoices in the truth. It bears all things, believes all things, hopes all things, endures all things. Love never ends. But as for prophecies, they will come to an end; as for tongues, they will cease; as for knowledge, it will come to an end. For we know only in part; but when the complete comes, the partial will come to an end. When I was a child, I spoke like a child, I thought like a child, I reasoned like a child; when I became an adult, I put an end to childish ways. For now we see in a mirror dimly, but then we will see face to face. Now I know only in part; then I will know fully, even as I have been fully known. And now faith, hope, and love abide, these three; and the greatest of these is love." (1 Corinthians 13, NRSV)

The love chapter clearly compares and contrasts love with behavior that either demonstrates love or that is just the opposite of love. It provides a checklist of sorts to show Christians how "love" thinks, responds and forbears. Paul presents "love", according to his explanation of its attributes, as a key barometer for spiritual maturity. He describes all other behavior as childish.

The believer is challenged daily to let love rule in all thoughts and actions. The standard of love will subdue competitiveness, feelings of rejection, vengefulness, a sense of entitlement, fear, greed, jealousy and other human vices that thwart spiritual maturity. It is important that Christians think of God as a parent whose chief goal is to advance the Christian from spiritual childhood to spiritual adulthood by conforming God's children into Christ's image and likeness.

DIVINE STRATEGY

Prayer Focus: Loving God, help me to develop the agape love you require for spiritual maturity. Lead and guide me to desire the discipline you provide. Help me to grow toward this kind of love, so I can be all I can be for you in the world, knowing that no matter what I accomplish in life, nothing is greater than love. Amen.

Scripture Focus — 1 John 4:18, NRSV: "There is no fear in love, but perfect love casts out fear; for fear has to do with punishment, and whoever fears has not reached perfection in love."

REFLECTION

_____
_____
_____
_____
_____
_____
_____
_____
_____
_____
_____
_____
_____
_____
_____
_____
_____
_____
_____
_____
_____
_____

CHAPTER 7-26

The Holy Spirit: The Comforter

Life is filled with so many swift transitions and quick transactions. Because we live in a fallen world, we experience loss, sadness, sickness, disappointment, hurt, pain, rejection and the wide of array of emotions. Therefore, in addition to the Spirit of truth, the Holy Spirit is also a comforter.

After Christ's death, burial and Resurrection, he left The Holy Spirit to lead, guide and direct believers as an indwelling presence that gives us a divine nature, if received and accepted. Christ knew sometimes our souls would need to be comforted. It is important to be able to recognize the Spirit of comfort and rely on it during times of adversity. John 14:16-18, NRSV, promises, "And I will ask the Father, and he will give you another Advocate, to be with you forever. This is the Spirit of truth, whom the world cannot receive, because it neither sees him nor knows him. You know him, because he abides with you, and he will be in you. I will not leave you orphaned; I am coming to you." So often, we look for comfort and peace in circumstances. We rely on networks and other external forces to provide comfort. We should care for one another and support each other in the time of trouble. Yet, the comfort of others is not as complete as the power of the Holy Spirit. Often, Satan torments in the dark hours of night when friends and loved ones may not be available. The sheer magnitude of some situations can cause tremendous stress that leads to desperate decision making. The Spirit of comfort attacks the lies and torment and brings the peace that allows rest and sleep. God's word facilitates our ability to draw upon the Spirit of comfort.

Take the time to quiet your soul and allow the Spirit of comfort to assure you that you are accepted in the beloved, that God will exchange your yoke of heaviness for a yoke of ease, that God is a friend when others forsake you. Connect to the Holy Spirit within you and know God cares for you.

DIVINE STRATEGY

Prayer Focus: Loving God, I acknowledge the Holy Spirit within me that teaches me the truth and comforts me in the time of trouble. Help me to remember I have a constant friend in the person of the Holy Spirit so that no matter what happens, my soul will not experience despair. Amen.

Scripture Focus — John 14:25-27, NRSV: "'I have said these things to you while I am still with you. But the Advocate, the Holy Spirit ... will teach you everything, and remind you of all that I have said to you. Peace I leave with you; my peace I give to you. I do not give to you as the world gives. Do not let your hearts be troubled, and do not let them be afraid.'"

REFLECTION

_____

_____

_____

_____

_____

_____

_____

_____

_____

_____

_____

_____

_____

_____

_____

_____

_____

CHAPTER 7-27

The Believer's Identity

Nips, tucks, liposuction, plastic surgery, lotions, potions, creams, weight-loss diets, diet pills, "miracle" herbs and supplements are a few of the items on a seemingly inexhaustible list of quick fixes for either slowing the aging process or enhancing physical appearance. Consumers of these products and services spend millions of dollars annually to "look the part" and boost self-confidence and self-esteem. People search for a sense of identity by improving or changing themselves outwardly.

Yet, even with all the medical and technological advances available, never before have so many seemed unsure of who they are inwardly. Even believers are plagued by doubt and a sense of uncertainty of their identity.

The Bible, the Word of God, is the only mirror that can provide truthful responses to the compelling questions, "Who am I?" and "What is my purpose in life?" The Holy Scriptures contain very specific descriptions and validation for the identity of the believer. Jesus Christ himself is the model for how to connect with God for gaining certainty about identity. The Pharisees and other biblical characters Jesus encountered often asked him who he was and why he was on earth. "So the Jews gathered around him and said to him, 'How long will you keep us in suspense? If you are the Messiah, tell us plainly'" (John 10:24, NRSV). Jesus replied, "The Father and I are one" (John 10:30, NRSV). "I came down from heaven not to follow my own whim but to accomplish the will of the One who sent me" (John 6:38, The Message).

Throughout the New Testament, which includes chronicles of the life and times of Jesus Christ, never was Jesus confused about his identity. He never sought the approval of the rabbinical priests. He never wavered in his understanding and acceptance that he was the Son of God sent from God to save the world. Jesus only sought to please God and to gain God's approval. God affirms Christ in the well-known passage, "And a voice from heaven said, 'This is my Son, the Beloved, with whom I am well pleased" (Matthew 3:17, NRSV).

The beauty of having Jesus as a model for us as Christians to know and accept our identity is that Jesus does for believers what God did for him. He assures us as believers that we are fearfully and wonderfully made, loved and accepted, redeemed, covered, forgiven, protected, empowered, overcoming, victorious and delivered. When we as Christians meditate on these God-given components of our identity, we become more confident and less reliant on external foundations upon which to build identity. In relationship, we can look to God the Creator, God the Redeemer and God the Sustainer to validate us and provide a sense of self-worth. We can know that whether life experiences are good or bad, we are the righteousness of God in Christ Jesus.

DIVINE STRATEGY

Prayer Focus: Loving God, I am so thankful that you gave me identity so I don't have to wonder who I am or what I should do. You have made it so clear in your word that like Jesus, I am your child and you created me to fulfill the purpose you assigned to me. Help me to believe and accept your divine will and purpose for my life and to know you came so I might have life more abundantly. Create in me the calm assurance that I do not have to perform, overachieve, or look or behave in a certain way in order to be approved by you. Yet, give me the wisdom to grow in favor with God and humanity. Amen.

Scripture Focus — 1 Peter 4:14, NRSV: "If you are reviled for the name of Christ, you are blessed, because the Spirit of glory, which is the Spirit of God, is resting on you."

REFLECTION

CHAPTER 7-28

A Divine Appointment

Have you ever met a stranger who offered you profound advice? Were you ever invited to attend what you thought would be an ordinary luncheon, dinner or event that turned out to be extraordinary? Or have you ever received a phone call from a long-lost friend, only to discover that these seemingly "chance" encounters were not by chance at all? In fact, many times these encounters are filled with opportune and necessary information, encouragement or whatever is needed during the time of the experience. Before long, you're thinking to yourself, "Wow! I wasn't expecting that!" When these experiences happen in my life, I call them divine appointments.

God speaks in a variety of ways. God often enters believer's everyday lives through real people we may not even know, but who are willing to be vessels God can use. When believers pray and ask God for solutions to problems, sometimes we also ask for specific ways and means for delivering those solutions. But, often when believers consider logical ways to solve a problem, God may do something illogical.

God may work through a person you least expect to help. God may answer your needs by providing an opportunity for someone else to respond to the need, which is also an answer to their prayer. Divine appointments are not only surprising; they also cause a sensation of a divine presence that has orchestrated events and people to happen at just the right time. People often describe the feeling as a sense of being at the right place at the right time or they may exclaim, "I am supposed to be here" or "I was supposed to meet you today."

Scriptures substantiate God's use of divine appointments. God sent the prophet Elijah to the widow at Zarephath who was gathering sticks when he happened upon her. Because of a drought and famine in her area, she was about to prepare what she thought would be her last meal for her son and herself. However, Elijah instructed her to prepare the meal for him instead and then prophesied that her obedience to his instruction would cause the oil and flour to multiply and feed her and her son for many days (1 Kings 17, NRSV). Perhaps one of the most renowned divine appointments in Scripture is Jesus' encounter with the woman at the well. He came to the well in Samaria after a long journey, when a woman arrived to draw water. Jesus asked her to draw water for Him as well. Seeing that Jesus was a Jew, the woman was astounded that He was interacting with her. Jesus told her that if she really understood who He is, she would ask Him to give her living water. Jesus began to minister to the woman. She testified to other Samaritans about Jesus and they came to believe that He was the Messiah (John 4:5-42, NRSV).

Take time to think about your divine appointments. Reflect on the times you realized God was using you to bless another person or God was using another person to bless you.

Record the experiences in a journal and marvel at the way God participates in your life. Recognize the times God may be using you as a divine appointment for someone else and obey the leading of the Holy Spirit.

DIVINE STRATEGY

Prayer Focus: Loving God, thank you for the many divine appointments you have designed for my life. I recall events and coincidences that I chalked up as serendipities. However, I now see you orchestrated those events. Help me to remember and document any events and people whom you used to warn, protect, advise and even admonish me, all for my ultimate good. Help me to follow the leading of your Holy Spirit to be used as a divine appointment in someone else's life. Help me not to dismiss the urge to help, pray, call, bless, forgive, take to lunch, send a card or whatever you might ask me to do, even if, at first, I can't understand or explain why I feel called to do it. Most of all, help me to know you want me to join you where you are at work and in so doing, experience you in ways I may never imagine. Amen.

Scripture Focus — Hebrews 13:2, NSRV: "Do not neglect to show hospitality to strangers, for by doing that some have entertained angels without knowing it."

REFLECTION

_____

_____

_____

_____

_____

_____

_____

_____

_____

_____

_____

_____

_____

_____

WALKING IN DIVINE FAITH AND PEACE

Throughout life, believers face challenges and times when faith is tested. Often, believers feel powerless to get through circumstances without bouts of fear and panic.

Faith and peace are two of God's favorite strategies for endurance in a crisis. Faith is substantive, and peace is an anchor to help the believer remain steadfast in the knowledge that God will work all things together for good.

Walking in divine faith and peace is definitely a fruit produced in a mature believer. With a commitment to exercise faith and peace in every circumstance, no matter what the situation may appear to be, what others say, or even the feelings that emotions evoke, soon the believer will experience a new level of glory and relationship with God.

The strategies in this chapter encourage the believer to formulate prayers that help strengthen faith and peace.

CHAPTER 8-29

Keep the Faith

I remember the first time I read Hebrews 11:1, NRSV, as a girl, "Now faith is the assurance of things hoped for, the conviction of things not seen." I read it over and over, trying to grasp the concept of faith as a tangible substance that could be used to create that which I could only imagine. Later, in my young adult life, I would read the Scripture and marvel at the arrangement of the words according to the apostle Paul and think, "Only a Sovereign God could inspire a mere mortal to conceive and make such a prolific statement." Yet, the full meaning was still somewhat obscure to me.

Life experience and middle age have afforded me the privilege of understanding better how faith itself has the power to make dreams manifest in reality. I have learned that faith begins with a thought that produces words of proclamation or declaration about a desired result and ends with the realization of exactly what I thought and stated. For believers, sometimes our only available resource is faith. The unpredictability of people and circumstances often leaves us feeling helpless and out of control. Only when we use our faith do we gain the wisdom needed to respond appropriately in every situation.

By faith, believers become better at solving problems. We are equipped to teach our children how to live by faith in the results they want as long as their desires conform to God's desires for them. God desires that we should prosper and be in good health, even as our souls prosper. God wants us to fulfill purpose in life. God has a good plan for us. God wants to complete the good work he has begun in us in all the roles we fulfill.

DIVINE STRATEGY

Prayer Focus: Loving God, comfort and guide me in the knowledge that I always should use faith to conquer any negative situation. Strengthen my ability to trust in you and to believe faith is powerful. Amen.

Scripture Focus — Mark 11:23, NRSV: "Truly I tell you, if you say to this mountain, 'Be taken up and thrown into the sea,' and you do not doubt in your heart, but believe that what you say will come to pass, it will be done for you."

REFLECTION

_____

_____

_____

_____

_____

_____

_____

_____

_____

_____

_____

_____

_____

_____

_____

_____

_____

_____

_____

_____

_____

_____

CHAPTER 8-30

Rest in God

One of my Dad's favorite spiritual sayings was, "Our extreme is God's opportunity." I remember being so comforted by those words. Now as a a married woman with children, when I feel that I have done as much as I can do to resolve issues, I still hear my Dad's calm and powerful voice giving me all the confidence I need to rest as I let God guide me in handling my situation.

Today, on my journey of faith, I can testify that when I have done all I can, standing in full assurance that God will work supernaturally to fix my circumstances, God has come through every time. Throughout the Holy Scriptures, which I often refer to as the "Love Letter" or "The Book of Promises", Christians are reminded that faith in God creates the energy needed to do the work of faith. Even if we are too tired to do the work of faith, God affords the grace to allow us to rest while God does the work. Jesus often spoke to multitudes of people who marveled at his words and miracles. They followed him as he traveled, hanging on to his words and being healed of their infirmities. The people Jesus encountered during his lifetime were burdened by sin and wearied by trying to keep the Mosaic laws. Often, they were confused about exactly how to live a holy life in their humanity. He said to them, "Come to me, all you that are weary and are carrying heavy burdens, and I will give you rest. Take my yoke upon you, and learn from me; for I am gentle and humble in heart, and you will find rest for your souls. For my yoke is easy, and my burden is light" (Matthew 11:28-30, NRSV). Jesus gave them a new strategy other than striving to deal with the complexities of life. He assured them they could trust in the omnipotent God to care for and cover them.

Jesus Christ made an amazing promise when he told his disciples he would leave them a comforter, the Holy Spirit, to teach them all truth, guide their decisions and help them to keep the commandments. He told them, "If you love me, you will keep my commandments. And I will ask the Father, and he will give you another Advocate, to be with you forever." (John 14:15-16, NRSV)

Jesus desires that believers stand in the knowledge that we do not have to handle life alone. Believers have divine help. Most of all, Jesus desires that Christians take the time to rest and look to him for the grace to leave our cares with him.

DIVINE STRATEGY

Prayer Focus: Loving God, I thank you for your perfect peace when I am tired and weary. I purpose to bring my burdens to you and leave them there. Amen.

Scripture Focus — Psalm 55:22, NRSV: "Cast your burden on the Lord, and he will sustain you; he will never permit the righteous to be moved."

REFLECTION

_____

_____

_____

_____

_____

_____

_____

_____

_____

_____

_____

_____

_____

_____

_____

_____

_____

_____

_____

_____

_____

_____

_____

CHAPTER 8-31

A Survivor Mentality

October has become nationally known as Breast Cancer Awareness Month. Every year, organizations and groups gather to celebrate survivors and commemorate those who succumbed in the fight. Education and outreach workshops designed to provide information and tools to prevent breast cancer abound.

Health fairs and free mammogram screenings have served to detect new cases of the disease for women who would have been unable to access health care. Survivors share their stories of courage in the face of pain and anxiety. For so many survivors, a renewed sense of self and a God-centeredness result from the experience.

So many breast cancer survivors have declared that breast cancer was the best thing that ever happened to them and that, because of their faith, they are able to look to God and see His divine provision and care. Later, as I reflected on their stories, I realized that they totally get it! Life is about having a survivor mentality, which is the faith not only to believe God will provide supernatural change or healing, but also to see areas of benefit in the situation. This kind of faith creates the optimal conditions for the body to heal itself and respond positively to the treatment.

In the Apostle Paul's letter to the Philippian church, he writes, "My dear, dear friends! I love you so much. I do want the very best for you. You make me feel such joy, fill me with such pride. Don't waver. Stay on track, steady in God. I urge Euodia and Syntyche to iron out their differences and make up. God doesn't want his children holding grudges. And, oh, yes, Syzygus, since you're right there to help them work things out, do your best with them. These women worked for the Message hand in hand with Clement and me, and with the other veterans — worked as hard as any of us. Remember, their names are also in the Book of Life. Celebrate God all day, every day. I mean, revel in him! Make it as clear as you can to all that you meet that you're on their side, working with them and not against them. Help them see that the Master is about to arrive. He could show up any minute! Don't fret or worry. Instead of worrying, pray. Let petitions and praises shape your worries into prayers, letting God know your concerns. Before you know it, a sense of God's wholeness, everything coming together for good, will come and settle you down. It's wonderful what will happen when Christ displaces worry at the center of your life. Summing it all up, friends, I'd say you'll do best by filling your minds and meditating on things true, noble, reputable, authentic, compelling, gracious — the best, not the worst; the beautiful, not the ugly; things to praise, not things to curse. Put into practice what you learned from me, what you heard and saw and realized. Do that, and God, who makes everything work together, will work you into his most excellent harmonies. I'm glad in God, far happier than you would ever guess — happy that you're again showing such strong concern for me. Not that you ever quit praying and thinking about me. You just had no chance to show it. Actually, I don't have a sense of needing anything personally. I've learned by now to be quite content whatever my circumstances. I'm just as happy with little as with much, with much as with little. I've found the recipe for being happy whether full or hungry, hands full or hands empty. Whatever I have, wherever I am, I can make it through anything in the One who makes me who I am." (Philippians 4:1-13, The Message)

A survivor mentality requires believers to be steadfast and immovable in the face of trials. Like the apostle Paul, believers must learn how to be abased and how to abound because the strengthening power of Christ gives us the grace to do all things. The courageous woman with breast cancer understands this principle, and she is able to find peace, knowing God will meet her needs in every way!

DIVINE STRATEGY

Prayer Focus: Loving God, help me to learn the power of standing firmly in faith regardless of my circumstances. Help me to acquire the strength to all things through Christ. Amen.

Scripture Focus — Psalm 28:7, NRSV: "[God] is my strength and my shield; in him my heart trusts; so I am helped, and my heart exults, and with my song I give thanks to him."

REFLECTION

_____

_____

_____

_____

_____

_____

_____

_____

_____

_____

_____

_____

_____

_____

_____

_____

_____

_____

_____

_____

_____

_____

Heaven Never Shuts Down

News headlines heralded the message, "U.S. government shut down as Congress can't agree on spending bill." The House and Senate came to a total deadlock on issues and amendments related to the President's health-care plan. Twenty-five percent of 3.3 million "non-essential" federal employees were furloughed indefinitely, until a workable agreement could be reached. Americans continued to suffer the adverse effects of a "house divided".

Thanks to God, believers can enjoy the calm assurance that heaven never shuts down. God the Creator, God the Redeemer, God the Sustainer and the host of angels are always in agreement, and they are available around the clock to ensure the safety, security and protection of God's children. These are perilous times; yet, Christians have divine protection. The fear of loss of income and financial stability can loom large when economic downturns and government upheaval predict a bleak outlook. It is important for Christians to remember that help comes from God, the source of all provisions.

Trust and rely on the promises of God in troubled times. Meditate on Psalm 27:1, The Message: "Light, space, zest — that's God! So, with him on my side, I'm fearless, afraid of no one and nothing". Be comforted by Christ's proclamation in John 14:27, NRSV. "Peace I leave with you; my peace I give to you. I do not give to you as the world gives. Do not let your hearts be troubled, and do not let them be afraid." Fortify your minds with this powerful instruction in Philippians 4:6-8, NRSV. "Do not worry about anything, but in everything by prayer and supplication with thanksgiving let your requests be made known to God. And the peace of God, which surpasses all understanding, will guard your hearts and your minds in Christ Jesus." So, no matter what is going on, always remember that heaven never shuts down. God's promises are always true. God's mercies are new every morning, and the government is on God's shoulders.

DIVINE STRATEGY

Prayer Focus: Loving God, I choose to rest in knowledge that you will supply all of my needs according to your riches in glory, and that since my house is built upon the rock, I can be assured that the rains and storms of life will not destroy it. Amen.

Scripture Focus — Jeremiah 17:7-8, The Message: "But blessed is the man who trusts me, God, and the woman who sticks with God. They're like trees replanted in Eden, putting down roots near the rivers — Never worry through the hottest of summers, never dropping a leaf, Serene and calm through droughts, bearing fresh fruit every season."

REFLECTION

_____

_____

_____

_____

_____

_____

_____

_____

_____

_____

_____

_____

_____

_____

_____

_____

_____

_____

_____

CHAPTER 9

WALKING IN DIVINE PURPOSE

In today's world, especially in a capitalistic society, many regard purpose in life as closely related to earning profits. However, God's divine purpose for the life of the believer may require the sacrifice of an opulent lifestyle for one of comfort and sharing, giving to the poor or interacting with people and circumstances that high society standards would require they exclude.

The strategies for walking in divine purpose presented in this chapter challenge the believer to realize attitudes and deeds toward the least are what Christ came to exemplify. God's redemptive plan and purpose include the salvation and uplifting of all sinners. God uses people to carry out God's plans and purposes on the earth. With a willing heart and mind, the believer can come to know God and appreciate life in ways money cannot buy.

CHAPTER 9-33

The Purpose of Life

"It's all about the Benjamins" is a common vernacular phrase in today's world to describe the motivation for time spent to produce income and sometimes, to justify the means used for producing income. This mindset suggests that the primary purpose in life is to pursue and achieve great wealth. It is the standard by which even some Christians have come to measure their success and ability to be respected among their peers. This mindset is all too often the most prevalent motivation for activity of any kind. "How can I get to know the right people?" "What can I do to be selected for or to create the most lucrative opportunity?" "What must I compromise to be viewed as being at the top of my game?" As these types of questions flood the mind and drive decision making and choices, the quest for God's purpose for life looms vaguely, if at all, in the distant background.

The Bible clearly ordains, confirms and commands work in order to provide for self and families. In fact, due to the fall of humanity, God pronounced work as one of the results of the sin of eating of the tree of the knowledge of good and evil. "And to the man he said, 'Because you have listened to the voice of your wife, and have eaten of the tree about which I commanded you, 'You shall not eat of it,' cursed is the ground because of you; in toil you shall eat of it all the days of your life; thorns and thistles it shall bring forth for you; and you shall eat the plants of the field. By the sweat of your face you shall eat bread until you return to the ground, for out of it you were taken; you are dust, and to dust you shall return'" (Genesis 3:17-19, NRSV). Therefore, spending time working to eat is a part of the plight of the human experience.

In the person of Jesus Christ is a man who worked as a carpenter. Yet, we find little to no mention of Jesus' profession or any emphasis on how he spent his time producing income. Rather, Jesus used his profession not only to participate in the human experience while on earth, but also to demonstrate that his true purpose in life was to build people and help them construct their lives so they could receive and accept the truth of the redemption he ultimately would provide. The Bible does not portray Jesus as focusing on meeting the "head honcho," "hobnobbing" with the right crowd or being "on top of his game" as a master craftsman in the marketplace in order to get ahead. Yet, this is not to say Jesus was not excellent in his craft or did not care about the quality of his work. Nor is it to say that as modern-day believers, we should ignore sensible strategies to live successfully in a capitalistic society.

However, Jesus clearly states in John 6:38, The Message: "I came down from heaven not to follow my own whim but to accomplish the will of the One who sent me." In the apostle Paul's letter to the Philippians (2:6-8, NRSV) he describes Jesus as "who, though he was in the form of God, did not regard equality with God as something to be exploited, but emptied himself, taking the form of a slave, being born in human likeness. And being found in human form, he humbled himself and became obedient to the point of death — even death on a cross." Jesus knew and understood his purpose within the context of his work. He did not see his work alone as the fulfillment of his purpose.

Modern authors such as Rick Warren, author of *The Purpose Driven Life*, and Henry Blackaby, author of *Experiencing God: Knowing and Doing the Will of God*, present inspiring perspectives on how to see God as pursuing the kind of relationship with believers that causes them to choose God's will in exchange for choosing their own will. Blackaby's concept of the "Seven Realities of Experiencing God" offers a unique and effective perspective on understanding the will of God and how God wants to work through the lives of believers:

1. God is always at work around you.
2. God pursues a continuing love relationship with you that is real and personal.
3. God invites you to become involved in God's work.
4. God speaks by the Holy Spirit, through the Bible, prayer, circumstances and the church (other believers).
5. God's invitation for you to work with God always leads you to a crisis of belief that requires faith and action.

6. You must make major adjustments in your life to join in what God is doing.
7. You come to know God by experience as you obey and God accomplishes work through you.

These perspectives challenge believers to reframe their entire motivation for working and living. The goal to produce high levels of income by any means necessary and to acquire status among peers was not included in God's will and purpose for the life of Christ, nor is it included in God's will and purpose for the life of believers. Although God gives the power to create wealth for the purpose of providing resources to advance the church's mission, God calls and ordains whom God wills to possess the power of wealth. God requires total submission in the use of it. God wants to do so much in the world through the life of the believer. Take time from the hustle and bustle of life to quiet your soul and allow God to reveal God's will and purpose for using your life. Then, allow God to give you the courage to humble yourself to God's will and purpose. You may be surprised at just how fulfilling and rich your life will become!

DIVINE STRATEGY

Prayer Focus: Loving God, give me the mind of Christ to learn and fulfill your purpose and will for my life. Help me to be open to a redirected career, a friendship or a relationship that perhaps I would not have chosen, a task you are asking me to complete, or the gift of unconditional love in a current relationship for which I do not feel positive emotions. Help me to discover where you are at work and to offer my life sacrificially to join you in that work, and thus experience a fulfillment like none I have ever known. Amen.

Scripture Focus — John 15:16, NRSV: "You did not choose me but I chose you. And I appointed you to go and bear fruit, fruit that will last, so that [God] will give you whatever you ask ... in my name."

REFLECTION

_____
_____
_____
_____
_____
_____
_____
_____
_____
_____
_____
_____
_____
_____
_____
_____
_____
_____
_____

CHAPTER 9-34

Divine Hospitality

The story of the Good Samaritan has always been one of my favorite biblical stories. As many times as I have read it, I never understood its full meaning until recently as I studied the story as part of an assignment in a ministry class.

This parable, told in the gospel according to Luke, is very poignant. Luke 10:25-37, NRSV, tells the story.

"Just then a lawyer stood up to test Jesus. "Teacher," he said, "what must I do to inherit eternal life?" He said to him, "What is written in the law? What do you read there?" He answered, "You shall love the Lord your God with all your heart, and with all your soul, and with all your strength, and with all your mind; and your neighbor as yourself." And he said to him, "You have given the right answer; do this, and you will live."

But wanting to justify himself, he asked Jesus, "And who is my neighbor?" Jesus replied, "A man was going down from Jerusalem to Jericho, and fell into the hands of robbers, who stripped him, beat him, and went away, leaving him half dead. Now by chance a priest was going down that road; and when he saw him, he passed by on the other side. So likewise a Levite, when he came to the place and saw him, passed by on the other side. But a Samaritan while traveling came near him; and when he saw him, he was moved with pity. He went to him and bandaged his wounds, having poured oil and wine on them. Then he put him on his own animal, brought him to an inn, and took care of him. Then the next day he took out two denarii, gave them to the innkeeper, and said, 'Take care of him; and when I come back, I will repay you whatever more you spend.' Which of these three, do you think, was a neighbor to the man who fell into the hands of the robbers?' He said, "The one who showed him mercy." Jesus said to him, "Go and do likewise."

In Matthew 25:34-40, NRSV, there is a similar parable. "Then the king will say to those at his right hand, 'Come, you that are blessed by my Father, inherit the kingdom prepared for you from the foundation of the world; for I was hungry and you gave me food, I was thirsty and you gave me something to drink, I was a stranger and you welcomed me, I was naked and you gave me clothing, I was sick and you took care of me, I was in prison and you visited me.' Then the righteous will answer him, 'Lord, when was it that we saw you hungry and gave you food, or thirsty and gave you something to drink? And when was it that we saw you a stranger and welcomed you, or naked and gave you clothing? And when was it that we saw you sick or in prison and visited you? And the king will answer them, 'Truly I tell you, just as you did it to one of the least of these who are members of my family, you did it to me.'"

The most important message in this parable is that the ministry of help and hospitality is so important to God that those who notice, stop, help, feed, clothe, visit, comfort and shelter a wounded stranger will inherit the kingdom of God. Today, "wounded strangers" can be found in many forms. They can be homemakers, overwhelmed by the demands of a young family. They can be homeless people begging on the corner. Or they can be great men and women with all of the trappings of success, with hearts crying for help with their inner turmoil.

With busy schedules and families to support, do we take the time to notice wounded strangers? Do we take a good look at the faces of people around us whose smiles may look out of place long enough to trace the tracks of their tears? Realize that of everything we do, what we do for others in need is the most important accomplishment to God.

DIVINE STRATEGY

Prayer Focus: Loving God, when I feel unsuccessful and unnoticed, help me to remember that providing help to those in need is the greatest accomplishment and that when I am thinking about all that I cannot do, help me to focus on that which I can do that means more to you. Amen.

Scripture Focus — Matthew 25:45-46, NRSV: "Then he will answer them, 'Truly I tell you, just as you did not do it to one of the least of these, you did not do it to me.' And these will go away into eternal punishment, but the righteous into eternal life."

REFLECTION

_____
_____
_____
_____
_____
_____
_____
_____
_____
_____
_____
_____
_____
_____
_____
_____
_____
_____
_____
_____

CHAPTER 10

SPIRITUAL WARFARE: THE MOST POWERFUL DIVINE STRATEGY

Waking the Dead by John Eldredge removed all confusion from my mind about the role of the enemy in the life of the believer. In one sentence, John provides the framework I needed for understanding the phenomenon of good and evil and how it plays out. "We-are-at-war!" This proclamation rang out at me with the rat-a-tat-tat 4/4 timing of a drum. For days, my thoughts remained focused on that one sentence. "We-are-at-war"! All the sudden, "putting on the whole armor of God", "believers having an adversary", "wrestling not with flesh and blood", "faith is the victory that overcomes", and other such Scriptural admonitions made perfect sense for the first time in my Christian walk. Believers are in a daily war with the enemy for our souls! By using the arrows of doubt and unbelief, and throwing daggers of fear and defeat, the enemy's goal is to wound the believer fatally until there is a cry of surrender to the wiles of the enemy. I finally realized the necessity of spiritual warfare.

The divine strategies presented in this last chapter should lead the believer to begin engaging in spiritual warfare with the keen understanding that God equips the believer to win the battle.

CHAPTER 10-35

Life Is War

Have you ever gone into a mall seeking a particular store, and after looking left and right at all of the stores lining both sides of the vast edifice, thought, "Where am I in proximity to where I am trying to go?" Did you then go to the mall directory, which is a simple schematic of the name of each store arranged in alphabetical or numerical order by store type and location, to see where you were? There, the reassuring words "YOU ARE HERE" glared boldly, and with a sigh of relief, you gained the perspective you needed to reach your destination with confidence. Life can often feel much like this.

There comes a time in every Christian's life when we feel lost and unsure of where we are and where to go. Bills are due. Children may be off course. The doctor may have discovered you have a life-threatening disease. You are experiencing difficulties at work. You may even have been affected by a layoff. A troubled marriage or divorce may have blindsided you like a speeding car whizzing by from out of nowhere. Your question then becomes, "Where am I, and how on earth did I get here?"

The Bible tells us we have an adversary and life is war. Until we enter eternal life, we are in a never-ending fight for our lives. Because many Christians do not recognize they are in a war zone, they don't know what to do or what is happening. It is important to realize the enemy came to kill, steal and destroy, and Jesus came that we might have life more abundantly. If we are at war, then we must understand our opponent is Satan. We must understand what kind of war we face. We are in a spiritual war. Ephesians 6:12, NRSV, says, "For our struggle is not against enemies of blood and flesh, but against the rulers, against the authorities, against the cosmic powers of this present darkness, against the spiritual forces of evil in the heavenly places." We must have the right weapons. "For the weapons of our warfare are not merely human, but they have divine power to destroy strongholds" (2 Corinthians 10:4a, NRSV). Our armor must protect our vital organs. The helmet of salvation protects the head. The breastplate of righteousness protects our hearts and allows us to know who we are in Christ. The shield of faith allows us to quench the fiery darts of the wicked. The belt of truth helps us process facts. Most of all, we must be armed with the sword of the spirit which is the Word of God.

In a spiritual war, we must have a spiritual weapon, and the strategy to win is to speak the word over our circumstances. To financial hardship, speak, "And my God will supply every need of yours according to his riches in glory in Christ Jesus" (Philippians 4:19, NRSV). To the wayward child, speak, "Point your kids in the right direction — when they're old they won't be lost" (Proverbs 22:6, The Message). To the diagnosis of disease speak, "By his bruises we are healed" (Isaiah 53:5b, NRSV). To difficulties at work, speak, "The king's heart is a stream of water in the hand of the Lord" (Proverbs 21:1a, NRSV). To the troubled marriage or new divorce, speak "Therefore what God has joined together, let no one separate" (Mark 10:9, NRSV).

DIVINE STRATEGY

Prayer Focus: Loving God, thank you for letting me know where I am and how to handle my circumstances effectively. Help me to remember to use the WORD to fight my battles so that I will win. Amen.

Scripture Focus — Mark 11:23, NRSV: "Truly I tell you, if you say to this mountain, 'Be taken up and thrown into the sea,' and if you do not doubt in your heart, but believe that what you say will come to pass, it will be done for you."

REFLECTION

_____

_____

_____

_____

_____

_____

_____

_____

_____

_____

_____

_____

_____

_____

_____

_____

_____

_____

_____

_____

_____

_____

CHAPTER 10-36

Give No Place to Fear

In today's world, believers are surrounded by news and information that incite spirits of fear that can eventually paralyze even the bravest of souls. Constant attacks from the enemy on minds and hearts create a sense of dread and impending catastrophe. It is enough to cause panic attacks and all kinds of anxiety that can eventually produce physical maladies. How can believers protect themselves from feeling afraid and vulnerable in the face of so much talk?

Constant prayer and study of God's Word are the best two weapons for fighting fear and feeding faith. Memorization and recitation of powerful, specific Scriptures that tell how to handle fear is an important habit to form. The daily onslaught of bad news and unfortunate circumstances can damage the inner being emotionally and spiritually quite severely over time. The instructions, "fear not" and "be not afraid" are mentioned more than 100 times in the Bible. There is significant emphasis in the life of the Christian not to give in to the spirit of fear. As humans, however, fear is not only natural; it also is a necessary alert to signal possible danger or threat. It is important not to ignore emotions that are a part of the system for informing "fight-or-flight" instincts. However, spiritually, God promises to comfort and keep Christians in perfect peace no matter the circumstance. Tormenting fear that "something may happen, if ..." or "I'm afraid the aches and pains I am experiencing may be cancer" can keep the believer bound in a constant state of distress, which, in itself, really will cause harm.

A few Scriptures on how to handle fear will help drive fear away:

- "For God did not give us a spirit of cowardice, but rather a spirit of power and love and of self-discipline." (2 Timothy 1:7, NRSV)
- "Do not be afraid, little flock, for it is [God's] good pleasure to give you the kingdom." (Luke 12:32, NRSV)

- "The angel of [God] encamps around those who fear him, and delivers them." (Psalm 34:7, NRSV)
- "So do not be afraid; you are of more value than many sparrows." (Matthew 10:31, NRSV)
- "The Lord your God you shall follow, him alone you shall fear, his commandments you shall keep, his voice you shall obey, him you shall serve, and to him you shall hold fast." (Deuteronomy 13:4, NRSV)
- "Peace I leave with you; my peace I give to you. I do not give to you as the world gives. Do not let your hearts be troubled, and do not let them be afraid." (John 14:27, NRSV)
- "I hereby command you: Be strong and courageous; do not be frightened or dismayed, for ... your God is with you wherever you go." (Joshua 1:9, NRSV)
- "But even if you do suffer for doing what is right, you are blessed. Do not fear what they fear, and do not be intimidated." (1 Peter 3:14, NRSV)
- "One night the Lord said to Paul in a vision, 'Do not be afraid, but speak and do not be silent." (Acts 18:9, NRSV)
- "There is no fear in love, but perfect love casts out fear; for fear has to do with punishment, and whoever fears has not reached perfection in love." (1 John 4:18, NRSV)
- "When I am afraid, I put my trust in you." (Psalm 56:3, NRSV)

DIVINE STRATEGY

Prayer Focus: Loving God, help me to develop a spirit of love and trust to drive out the spirit of fear. Always remind me that you have a good plan for my life, to prosper me and allow me to be in good health, to bless me and to give me hope and a future. Amen.

Scripture Focus — 1 John 4:18, NRSV: "There is no fear in love, but perfect love casts out fear; for fear has to do with punishment, and whoever fears has not reached perfection in love."

REFLECTION

BIBILIOGRAPHY

Mary A. Baker, words; Horatio R. Palmer, music, "Master, the Tempest Is Raging" (1874).

Henry Blackaby, *Seven Realities of Experiencing God* (Nashville, TN: LifeWay, 2007).

Frances Hodgson Burnett, *The Secret Garden* (New York: Waldman Publishing Corp., 1911).

Wesley L. Duewel, *Mighty Prevailing Prayer* (Grand Rapids, MI: Zondervan, 1990).

John Eldredge, *Waking the Dead: The Glory of a Heart Fully Alive* (Nashville, TN: Thomas Nelson, Inc., 2006).

Duane Elmer, *Cross-Cultural Servanthood: Serving the World in Christlike Humility* (Downers Grove, IL: IVP Books —I nterVarsity Press, 2006).

Kate McVeigh, *Get Over It: Overcoming the Enemy's Strategy of Offense* (Tulsa, OK: Harrison House, 1999).

Watty Piper, *The Little Engine That Could* (New York, NY: Platt & Munk, Publishers, 1930).

William "Smokey" Robinson, Jr., Warren Moore, Marvin Taplin, words and music, "The Tracks of My Tears" (Tamla Records, 1965)

Gary Smalley, Al Janssen, *Joy That Lasts* (Grand Rapids, MI: Zondervan, 2002).

Charles Albert Tindley, words and music, "We'll Understand It Better By and By," 1906.

John F. Wade, words and music, "O Come, All Ye Faithful (1743).

Wallace, William Ross, "The Hand That Rocks the Cradle Is the Hand That Rules the World," 1865.

Rick Warren, *The Purpose-Driven Life* (Grand Rapids, MI: Zondervan, 2002).

Thomas Whitfield, "We Need a Word from the Lord" from "The New Gospel Legends: The Best of Thomas Whitfield." (Zomba Recording LLC: 1999).

Jennie Bain Wilson, lyrics "Hold to God's Unchanging Hand" music, Franklin L. Eiland, 1906.

CPSIA information can be obtained at www.ICGtesting.com
Printed in the USA
LVOW07s0110081115

461430LV00001B/2/P